heirloom knits

heirloom knits

20 Classic designs to cherish

Judith McLeod-Odell

COLLINS & BROWN

First published in the United Kingdom in 2007 by
Collins & Brown
151 Freston Road
London
W10 6TH

An imprint of Anova Books Company Ltd

Commissioning Editor Michelle Lo

Design Manager Gemma Wilson

Editor Marie Clayton

Designer Nicky Collings

Photographer Dan Duchars

Senior Production Controller Morna McPherson

Stylist Ella Bradley

Pattern checker Marilyn Wilson

Illustrator Kang Chen

Editorial Assistant Katie Hudson

ISBN: 978 1 84340 387 6

A CIP catalogue record for this book is available from the British Library.

10 9 8 7 6 5 4 3 2 1

Reproduction by Anorax
Printed and bound by Craft Print International Ltd, Singapore

This book can be ordered direct from the publisher.
Contact the marketing department, but try your
bookshop first.

www.anovabooks.com

Introduction

My grandmother taught me to knit during the Second World War. The first thing I learned was how to wind a skein of yarn, and we would do this in the family's air raid shelter, while waiting for the sirens to give the all-clear. Because materials such as knitting needles were almost nonexistent at the time, I was taught spool knitting with the use of goose quills, and the occasional odd bicycle spoke filed down.

By the time I was nine, I had learned to unravel wool and steam it straight to be re-used for darning socks, a job I loathed. Darned socks were hard to wear so it wasn't long before I began knitting my own socks on four needles. Soon after, I was taught about pressing techniques as well as the art of embellishment, primarily embroidery. It was during these formative years that I gained most of my knowledge and love for textile art.

Knitting has certainly evolved from when I picked up my first pair of needles. When I was younger, there was a great deal of interest in the social and economic changes that had affected the knitting industry. Here in England, not only did the importation of cotton during the colonial days of Queen Victoria's reign influence our way of life, but two world wars most certainly altered our attitudes and expectations. As knitting gained greater status, practical items gave way to more decorative and fashionable knitting ideas, and soon the craft lent itself to home décor as well as clothing.

With this book, my goal was to renew the importance of knitting as a craft by creating twenty designs, each of which represents a decade of social change. Most of the projects in the book include the style of knitting of a particular era as well as a few techniques unearthed from the past that may be of historical interest.

Moreover, the projects have been embellished, just as in the past, with decorative borders or edgings. Whether it be a design based on the netting from the Bosphorus or a project illustrating candlewicking technique, this book offers a number of forgotten techniques that will delight and inspire knitters today.

Knitting has made a comeback recently and recycling, which was necessary in the postwar era, has now become fashionable again because of today's concern with the environment. So attention has not only been given to the modern aspects of knitting but also to the different patterns and styles of the past, balanced with the vintage techniques and the yarn equivalency of a particular time. Moreover, I've included an Embellishments section at the back of the book with an assortment of intricate borders and edgings that you can use to knit into your own heirloom piece.

With this book, I hope to not only bring a feeling of the history behind each pattern, but also a feeling of passion for the art of knitting and needlecrafts. I hope you'll have some fun with these projects and techniques so that you too can create your own unique and personal projects to pass down from generation to generation. Happy knitting…

History of hand knitting

No one knows for sure where and when knitting originated, although its roots lie far in the past. Early examples of the craft have been found as far back as 4th century BC Egypt and Arabia. In many cultures at this time, knitting was male-dominated while the women would spin the wool.

Particular styles of knitting in the British Isles developed in areas such as the Yorkshire Dales and famously in the isles of Guernsey, and Jersey. The distinctive patterns that came from these coastal communities became renowned throughout the world and are still associated with those areas today.

Patterns in knitting can be traced back as early as the 9th century in Scotland, having been used in Aran garments. The Picts were known for their interwoven and coiled designs, and these patterns are reflected in the hand knitted garments of Aran today. Eventually, these traditional patterns became more and more distinctive and region-based as the trend moved down the east coast of Scotland and England and down the west coast of Scotland and Ireland. The patterns

following the east coast of Scotland and England tended to have horizontal and localized designs (usually identifying the fishing village the pattern originated from) based on the zigzag of coastal paths or the shape of ocean waves. The patterns that spread down the west coast of Scotland and Ireland often featured vertical designs reflecting a family's occupation (usually in the fishing industry).

Later, knitters – particularly those from the Aran isles – adapted these famous cable patterns and orally passed the knowledge of how this was done through the generations, since almost nothing was written down and few people in these communities could read or write.

As early as the 15th century, Fair Isle, a remote island between the Orkney and Shetland Islands, was already producing Fair Isle knitting patterns in colours and designs not only attributable to the natural dyes from the island but to the Spaniards stranded there from the Spanish Armada. Scandinavian influences may have also contributed to some of the designs,

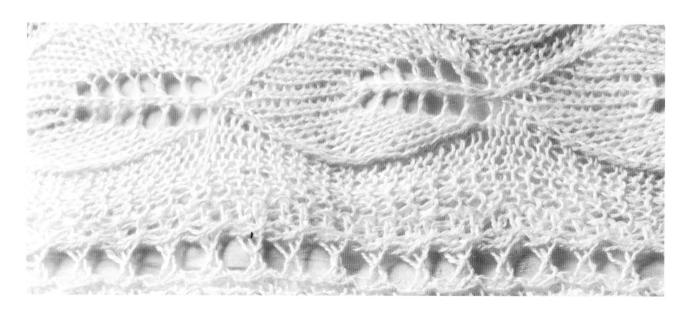

developed via the numerous trading links between Britain and the rest of Europe.

The Channel Islands were among the first to export their woollen clothing to England via France. It was also from these islands that the fishing industry was supplied with practical and warm clothing. From the isle of Jersey came the famous sweaters, which were originally invented out of the necessity for garments in which to work unencumbered. The chunky indigo-dyed woollen sweaters were knitted with their famous decorated edges and side slits for ease of movement. Similarly, Guernsey had its classic square-shaped woollen sweater with a straight neck, knitted on four or five needles, so that it could be reversed at any time in order to get further use out of the garment.

Shetland Lace developed in the Shetland Isles during the early years of the Victorian Era to accommodate the demand for lacy, feminine shawls and undergarments. The knitting technique is known to be knit on the bias and have neither a cast on nor cast off edge. The fineness of the knitted shawls was well known, and a mark of their quality was the fact that that they could be passed through a wedding ring. Each shawl is a work of art in itself and can take a year to produce, but the open work stitches that they invented are still in use today – a testament to the quality of the knitted work.

Among the more unusual developments was one that took place in the inland market town of Sanquhar about two hundred years ago. This knitting was distinguished by its two-coloured patterning, known as Sanquhar knitting, and it still flourishes today.

However, the popularity of knitting appeared to be directly related to the socio-economic environment of the times. In the 1700s, the textile trade was the second largest, after agriculture, in England and wool was used to make everything from clothes to interior goods. Cotton and linen were also widely used and were woven either as twill (fabric with a diagonal weave) or tabby (basic over and under) weave. However, during the turn of the century, the French and Industrial revolutions – as well as two World Wars in the twentieth century – caused the demise of the woollen trade between these islands and other countries, as far away as Canada. In England, yarn shortages also meant that during the First and Second World Wars knitting for the army and navy became more important than ever before (even knitted bandages in cotton could be made as part of the war effort). All other garments knitted for the family tended to be made of recycled yarn and, as a matter of course, learning to unpick and steam crinkly yarn was something all family members learned to do. Needles also were in short supply, so bicycle spokes would be filed down or goose quills used as alternatives. In fact, anything that the general public could get their hands on and which could be identified as a needle would be used to produce knitted garments.

Post-war influences, such as those of the film industry in Hollywood and America, as well as trends from Scandinavia, began to permeate not only the fashion industry but the interior design scene in Europe in the 1950s. This led to an improvement in the types of yarns and colours that were available and brought about better designs. This era also demanded strict adherence to knitting instruction manuals, books, and magazines.

The popularity of knitting began to wane and showed a sharp decline in the 1980s due to the perception of the craft as old fashioned. The increased availability of cheap machine-manufactured garments also had a marked effect, increasing this terminal decline. However, as the new millennium approached, knitting once again became fashionable and people everywhere started picking up their knitting needles – although this time it was not out of necessity but because it was seen as a satisfying and relaxing hobby that could yield unique and beautiful results.

In recent years, knitting is as popular as ever. This is in no small part due to fashion designers picking up on the trend for hand knitting and producing garments that are highly desirable. Magazines such as *Vogue Knitting* are also focusing on the production of knitting patterns and designs almost straight off the catwalk and Rowan Yarns offer not only high-quality knitting magazines and books suitable for the smartest coffee table, but new and exciting yarns that would have been undreamt of in previous eras.

Just as textile guilds several centuries before allowed the initiated to practise their crafts on a professional level, so universities more recently have begun to recognize the importance of knitting and are offering students a huge variety of different qualifications in textiles.

Celebrities have also played a part in the resurgence of knitting as a fashionable pastime, and widespread access to the internet has contributed to greater availability of knowledge, new ideas, and materials. This can quite clearly be seen through the involvement of entire countries globally in an exciting modernization of this very ancient craft. What still makes this historic craft so rewarding is the variety and creativity it offers for relatively little cost and effort. Even when working from a pattern the garment or item you produce will be different from any other.

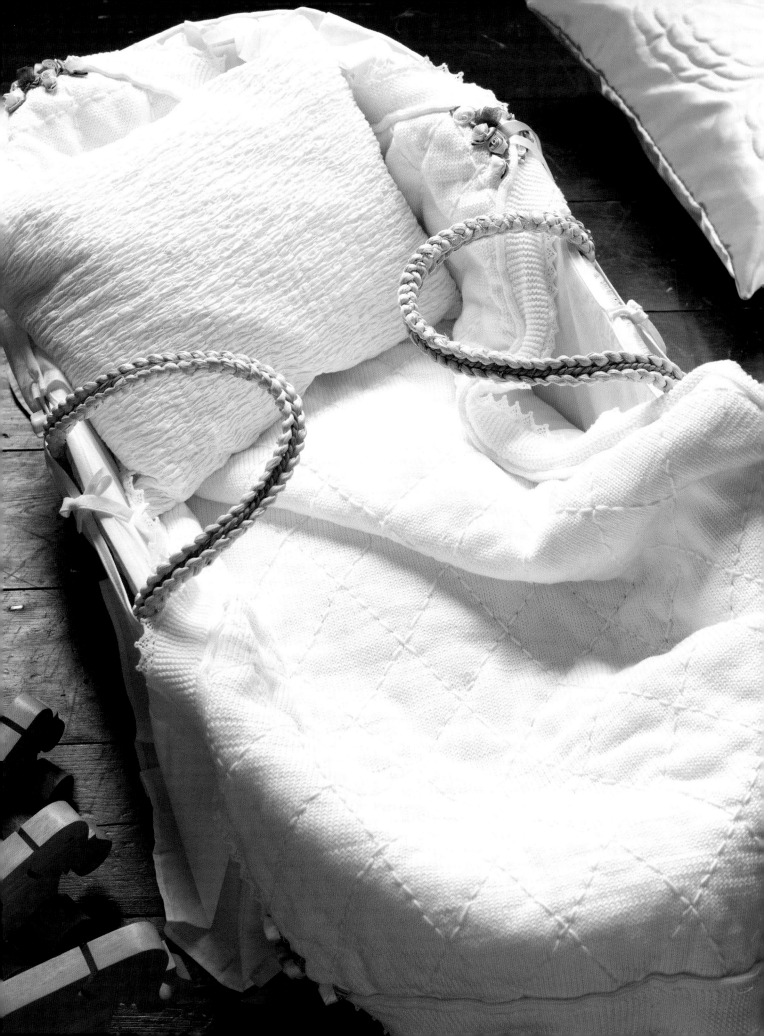

Basics

Yarns have changed a great deal since patterns first appeared. Some kinds of yarns, such as artificial silk have almost disappeared. There has also been a tendency to replace real wool and 100% cotton with mixes – and in some ways new, and modern yarns are far more challenging as far as tension or size of needles is concerned.

No modern yarns will be the equivalent to those given in very old patterns, since many old patterns recommend 2-ply and 3-ply yarns, which are difficult to find these days. It should be remembered that the old 2-ply and 3-ply yarns were thicker than the modern 2-ply and 3-ply yarns of today, but these patterns can quite often be knitted in today's 4-ply or even double knitting yarns. If the needle size is adjusted to keep the tension the same the knitter will notice that the garment will knit up the same, only with a slightly heavier texture.

Although a tension swatch is essential in most cases, breaking the rules that govern how people are first taught can lead to some exciting differences to knitting as a craft.

Most yarns and threads used for these crafts are categorized according to a scale of sizes, or weights. Terminology and weight vary slightly, although the most commonly used can be widely found. The following are some of the most commonly used plies:

2-ply and 3-ply yarns (Babyweight)

These are very fine yarns, used mainly for babies' garments and for lacy shawls. (Fine Shetland shawls are knitted from so-called '1-ply' yarn, but this is a misnomer, as at least 2 plies, or threads, are twisted together to form the yarn.) The recommended needle size for 2-ply and 3-ply yarns is 2.25mm–3.25mm (US 1–3).

4-ply yarns (Fingering)

These lightweight yarns work well for lacy garments and are available in a wide range of colours and various finishes. The recommended needle size for fingering yarns is 3.00–3.25mm (US 2–3).

DK (Double knitting or sport-weight)

This by far the most popular of the standard yarns. It can be used to make a huge range of garments and is suitable for most stitch patterns, from lace to heavily-textured. It also comes in a vast range of colours and in many finishes, from smooth to fluffy and tweed. The recommended needle size for DK or worsted yarns is 3.75mm–4.00mm (US 5–6).

Aran (Heavy worsted)

Somewhat heavier than double knitting, this is the yarn traditionally used for Aran garments and makes warm, durable knits. In the past traditional Aran yarns were available only in cream, but they can now be found in other colours. The recommended needle size for Aran yarns is 5.00–5.50mm (US 8–9).

Chunky (Bulky)

These thick yarns are generally used for loose-fitting outdoor sweaters and jackets and can have a smooth or brushed finish. The recommended needle size for chunky yarns is 6.00mm (US 10).

CHOOSING YARNS AND THREADS

When learning either knitting or crochet, it is especially important to choose a yarn that feels comfortable in your hands – one that is slightly elastic and neither too slippery nor so highly textured that it will not move smoothly between your fingers. A pure wool double knitting or Aran yarn is ideal for this purpose.

Published knitting and crochet patterns will usually specify the brand to be used for a project. You can often substitute a different yarn for the one specified, provided that you can obtain the same tension (see page 19), although substituting a different type of yarn – a textured yarn for a smooth one – will obviously produce a different appearance in the finished item.

When designing your own patterns, the only rule is: experiment. Try a stitch pattern with different weights and types of yarn and see the range of different effects you can create. With practise, you will learn which yarns are likely to enhance certain stitch patterns, but the occasional happy surprise will add to the fun of creating a new design.

Knitting equipment

Pairs of *needles* come in a wide range of sizes, from 2.00mm (US 0) to 19.00mm (US 35) in diameter (see below), and in various materials, including metal, plastic, wood, and bamboo; choose a type that you can

KNITTING		CROCHET HOOKS	
US	METRIC	US	METRIC
0	2.00mm	14 steel	0.60mm
1	2.25mm	12 steel	0.75mm
2	2.75mm	10 steel	1.00mm
3	3.25mm	6 steel	1.50mm
4	3.50mm	5 steel	1.75mm
5	3.75mm	B/1	2.25mm
6	4.00mm	C/2	2.75mm
7	4.50mm	D/3	3.25mm
8	5.00mm	E/4	3.50mm
9	5.50mm	F/5	3.75mm
10	6.00mm	G/6	4.00mm
10½	6.50mm	H/8	5.00mm
11	8.00mm	I/9	5.50mm
13	9.00mm	J/10	6.00mm
15	10.00mm	K/10½	6.50mm
17	12.75mm	L/11	8.00mm
19	15.00mm		
35	19.00mm		

knit with comfortably. Needles also come in several lengths, to accommodate different numbers of stitches.

Circular and *double-pointed needles* are designed mainly for knitting tubular or circular fabrics, although circular needles are also often used for flat knitting where many stitches are involved, since they can hold a great many stitches comfortably, with the weight of the work balanced between the two hands. Make sure that the length of a circular needle is at least 5cm (2in) less than the circumference of the work, which gives the minimum number of stitches required, at a given gauge, for the available lengths of circular needle.

Cable needles are short, double-pointed needles, used when moving groups of stitches, as in cabled or crossed-stitch patterns. They come in a just a few sizes; use one as close as possible to the working needle size, so that it will neither stretch the stitches nor slip out of the work. Those with a kink or a U-shaped bend are easier to work with than the straight kind.

Stitch holders resemble large safety pins. They are used to hold stitches that will be worked on later. Alternatively, a spare length of yarn can be threaded through the stitches and the ends knotted together. Where only a few stitches are to be held, an ordinary safety pin will do.

A *row counter* is a small cylindrical device with a dial used to record the number of rows, typically between working increases or decreases. Slip it over one needle before starting to knit and turn the dial at the end of each row.

Slip markers are used for marking the beginning of a round in circular knitting and sometimes for marking points in a stitch pattern.

A *needle gauge* is useful for checking the size of circular or double-pointed needles, which are not normally marked with their size, or for converting needle sizes.

You should have a few *crochet hooks* on hand for picking up dropped stitches, as well as for working the occasional crocheted edging for a knitted garment.

A *large tapestry or yarn needle* is used for sewing seams and has a blunt point, which will not split the yarn.

Dressmaker's pins are used for holding pieces of knitting or crochet together for sewing, for marking off stitches on a tension swatch, and also for pinning out pieces for blocking or pressing. Choose long ones with coloured heads. Large plastic, flat-headed pins, specially designed for use on knitted or crocheted fabrics, can be found in some places.

A *tape measure* is used for measuring tension and also the dimensions of knitted or crocheted fabric.

Small sharp-pointed *scissors* are another piece of essential equipment, used to cut the wool cleanly.

Small plastic *bobbins* are used for holding different-coloured yarns separate for some kinds of multicolour work.

A *calculator* is useful for figuring out the number of pattern multiples in a piece of knitting or the number of chains for crochet and is, of course, essential if you are creating your own design.

Graph paper is necessary when planning an original design.

TENSION

Tension or gauge most commonly refers to the number of stitches and rows obtained in a given stitch pattern worked over a given measurement – usually 10cm (4in). In a published knitting pattern, these figures will be stated, along with the recommended needles to be used.

Tension may also refer to the recommended number of stitches and rows, worked in stocking stitch, for a particular yarn: the number that will produce a pleasing fabric – neither too stiff, nor too loose and floppy. Often, this will be the same as the tension on a printed pattern using this yarn, at least where stocking stitch has been used as the standard.

Finally, there is the individual knitter's tension: the degree of tautness with which the yarn is held. Some people hold the yarn relatively loosely, which results in fewer stitches per cm (inch); others hold it more tightly, producing more stitches over the same measurement. There is no right and wrong here – what is important is to knit with an even tension, which remains the same over the piece of knitting, and, when following a pattern, to match the tension obtained by the pattern's designer.

Making a tension swatch

1. The tension given in a pattern will be over stocking stitch or the pattern stitch used for the garment. If it is given over a pattern stitch, it is necessary to cast on the correct multiple of stitches to be able to work the pattern. Whichever pattern stitch is used, cast on sufficient stitches to be able to work a swatch at least 12cm (5in) in width. Some patterns give the gauge over 5cm (2in), but a larger swatch gives a more accurate measurement. Knit a piece measuring approximately 12cm (5in) square, break the yarn, thread it through the stitches and slip them off the needle. Do not cast off or measure the swatch on the needle, as this may distort the stitches.

2. Take the stitch gauge by measuring horizontally across the centre of the sample where you have

relaxed a little after working the first few rows. Count the number of stitches stated in the pattern's recommended tension (for example, 20) and mark these with pins at either end. Take a ruler or tape measure and check the measurement between the pins; if your gauge is correct it should be 10cm (4in) (or whatever measurement the pattern states).

It is crucial to measure tension accurately; just half a stitch out over 10cm (4in) becomes quite a large inaccuracy over the full width of a garment or other knitted piece.

If the measurement between the pins is more than 10cm (4in), then your knitting is too loose; if it is less, your knitting is too tight. Make another swatch using smaller needles if your work is loose, or larger needles if it is tight. The needles stated in the pattern are the recommended size – it does not matter what size you use as long as you end up with the correct tension.

3. For the row tension count the number of rows recommended in the pattern vertically down the centre of the fabric. Mark with pins at each end, and then check the distance between them. (It is easier to count rows on the purl side of a stocking stitch or reverse stocking stitch fabric.) Once the stitch tension is right, the row tension is most likely to be correct. Any slight inaccuracies could be overlooked, as the lengthwise proportions of a garment are usually given as a measurement.

YARN SELECTION

For exact reproduction of the projects photographed, use the yarn listed in materials section of the pattern. Find your nearest yarn supplier in the resources listed on page 138.

YARN SUBSTITUTION

You may wish to try different yarns – perhaps it's an opportunity for you to use up leftovers from your yarn stash, or the yarn specified may not be available. You'll need to knit to the given tension to obtain the knitted measurements with a substitute yarn (see 'Tension' on page 19). In addition, be sure to consider how the fibre content of the substitute yarn will affect the comfort and the care of your projects.

After you've successfully swatched your substitute yarn, you'll need to determine how much of the new yarn the project requires. First, to find the total length of the original yarn in the pattern, multiply the number of balls by metres/yards per ball (listed on the ball band), then divide by the metres/yards per ball of the new yarn. Round up to the next whole number to find the number of balls of the new yarn required.

HOW TO KEEP LACE PATTERNS CORRECT

Complications often arise when a lace-patterned garment is shaped at the side edges – for example, when decreasing for the armhole. Unless row-by-row instructions are given, the knitter will have to use skill and judgement to keep the lace pattern correct. The following rules should help to keep your lace pieces looking as they should.

Most lace patterns rely on the fact that for every eyelet or hole made there is also a decrease. When shaping, you should regard these as pairs, and not work an eyelet without having enough stitches to work the decrease and vice versa. Check at the end of every row that you have the correct number of stitches, and that the eyelets and decreases are in the correct place above the previous pattern row. If there are insufficient stitches to work both the eyelet and the decrease, work the few stitches at either end in the background stitch (usually stocking stitch). When only a few stitches are to be decreased – say at an armhole or neck edge – insert a marker at the end of the first pattern repeat in from the edge. At the end of every decrease row check that there is the correct number of stitches in both these marked sections.

For large areas you may find that drawing the pattern and shaping on graph paper helps.

CORRECTING MISTAKES

Even the most experienced knitter makes the occasional mistake, but there are few mistakes that cannot subsequently be put right. There are, however, ways of avoiding mistakes, or seeing the error before you have worked too many rows above it. First, you can try out the stitch pattern in spare yarn before working the garment. In this way you will become familiar with the pattern and will be less likely to make a mistake. Secondly, while working the garment, check back after every pattern row to make sure the pattern has been worked correctly. It is far easier and less frustrating to unravel a few rows than half a garment.

pro

jects

Each of the twenty projects that follow takes its inspiration from a different decade, from the 1820s right up to the present. Whether you choose to knit an intricate Victorian-style floor rug or a sumptuous 1970s throw, the finished result is sure to be treasured for years to come.

Twining is thought to be of Swedish or German origin, dating back to the 14th century. The technique used here is a basic knit method with an interlacing filling yarn. It produces a dense and warm fabric, and boasts wonderful, delicate detail.

Twined cushion cover

THE ESSENTIALS

Measurements

40 x 40cm (16 x 16in)

Materials

Rowan *Big Wool Tuft*, 50g/1¾oz balls, approx 25m/27yd (wool)
    5 x Frost (A)

Rowan *Big Wool*, 100g/3½oz balls, approx 80m/87yd (wool)
    5 x White Hot (B)

10.00mm (US 15) needles

4.00mm (G/6) crochet hook

Leftover yarn or twine/or similar

40 x 40cm (16 x 16in) cushion pad

4 or more leather toggles

4 or more Medieval Knot closures (see right)

Tension

10 sts and 18 rows to 10cm (4in) over St st using 10.00mm (US 15) needles.

Note

Size of needle used can be varied. Although 15.00mm (US 19) needles are recommended for Big Wool, you may use 10.00mm (US 15) needles to produce a dense fabric with more durability. If you plan to use 15.00mm (US 19) needles, please follow the manufacturer's instructions for tension.

Stitches used

Garter Stitch
Reverse Stocking Stitch
Fancy Twined Stitch

Abbreviations

See page 136.

Fancy Twined Stitch pattern
Row 1 (RS): Using B p3, tie in A, leave B at front of work, * p3 using A, leave A at front of work, p3 using B; rep from * to last 3 sts, using A, p3.
(Note that each strand of yarn will be stranded every 3 sts along FRONT of work.)
Twist yarns together at end of each row.
Row 2 and 4 (WS): Using A k3, *k3 using B, k3 using A; rep from * across the row, stranding the yarn every 3 sts as before, this time at BACK of work (RS).
Row 3 (RS): Rep row 1.
Rows 5–10: Using B, knit. These 10 rows make up the Fancy Twined Stitch pattern. (By keeping the loops of yarn to one side and alternating each 3 sts with these two yarns, a twilling pattern will emerge.)

Knitting

Using B and 10.00mm (US 15) needles, cast on 54 sts and knit one row.
Cont in Fancy Twined Stitch pattern until desired length has been reached, ending with a (WS) row.
Cast (bind) off.

Making up

Sew up the sides to accommodate the cushion pad.

Medieval Knot closures

With brown twine or yarn, crochet or knit a fairly tight chain, approx 30cm (12in) long.
If the tension is too loose or sizing has changed, please adjust accordingly. To create the Medieval Knot closures, see diagram below. Sew toggles and Medieval Knots to open end of cushion. See photograph for placement.

MEDIEVAL KNOT
TOGGLE FASTENING

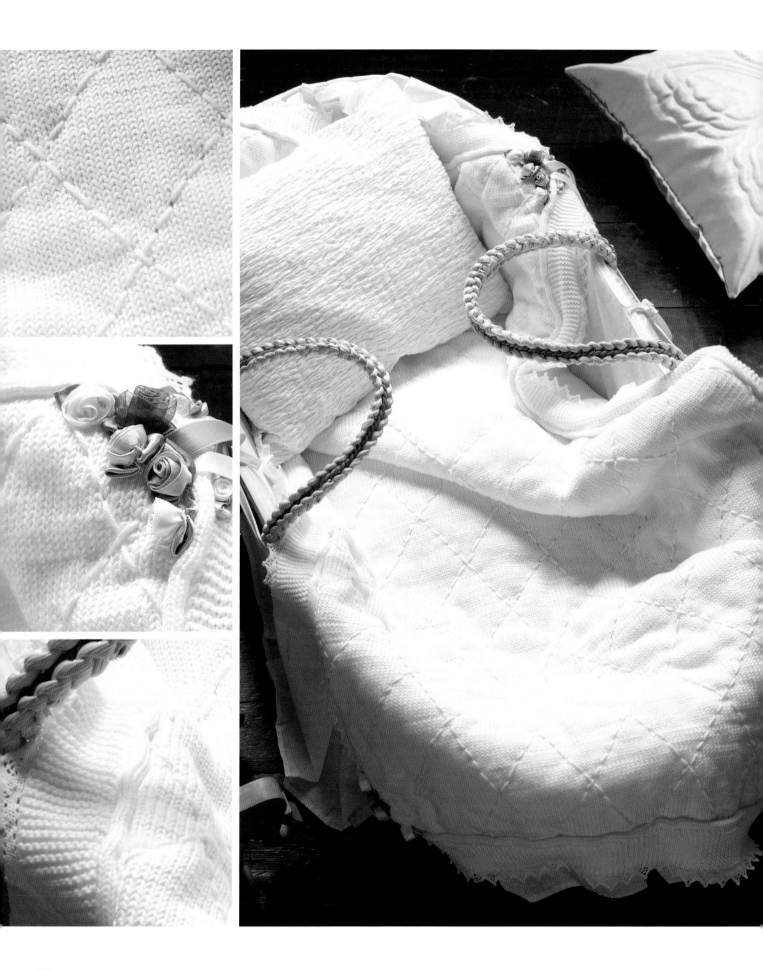

Quilting was developed when our ancestors realized that three layers of fabric were warmer than one. A piece of knitted cotton fabric is quilted to wadding, then accented with piping and various knitted embellishments.

Quilted baby blanket

THE ESSENTIALS

Measurements
60 x 108cm (24 x 43in) without edging

Materials
Rowan *Cotton Glacé*, 50g/1¾oz balls, approx 115m/125yd (cotton)
   10 x White (A)

Rowan *4-ply Cotton*, 50g/1¾oz balls, approx 170m/185yd (cotton)
   10 x White (B)

Rowan *Hand Knit Cotton*, 50g/1¾oz balls, approx 85m/92yd (cotton)
   1 x Bleached (C)

4.00mm (US 6) needles

3.25mm (US 3) needles

Pins

Non-permanent marking pen

Steel or rigid ruler

Wadding max tog 4, cut to size

Needle

Cotton for tacking

Tapestry needle

Knitted straight binding (optional)

3.75m (4¼yd) piping (optional)

Lace edgings/embellishments from a choice given on pages 110–129

Lining fabric, approx 60 x 108cm (24 x 43in)

Tension
22–24sts and 30 rows to 10 cm (4in) over St st using 4.00mm (US 6) needles.

Stitches used
Stocking Stitch
Garter Stitch
Backstitch for quilting

Abbreviations
See page 136.

Knitting
With yarn A and 4.00mm (US 6) needles, cast on 150 sts.
Knit in St st for 106cm (42½in) or length desired.
Cast (bind) off.

Quilting
Pin and press the knitted piece well with damp cloth. Leave pinned out before and during the marking off for quilting.

Using the non-permanent marking pen, mark off each of all four sides at 5cm (2in) intervals. Using ruler and pen, join each mark either diagonally for diamonds or crossways for squares. These intervals can be altered to suit.

Next turn the knitted piece onto WS, place wadding on top and cut it to fit close inside the edge of the knitting. Pin carefully all round the edges, through the two thicknesses, to hold the wadding in place and tack, starting from the centre, always working outwards to cover the entire piece of fabric.

Now with RS facing, thread the yarn needle with yarn C. Remembering to stitch both wadding and knitted fabric together, stitch along all the lines of the diamonds and round the edges as evenly as possible using either a running or

backstitch. Although hand stitching is used here for the authentic look, the fabric could also be machine quilted.

Press lightly using a damp cloth, steam with the iron (do not apply pressure with the iron) and keep pinned out until the next stage.

Making straight binding
Using B and 3.25mm (US 3) needles, cast on 8–10 sts depending on width of piping being used.

Work in St st and knit enough straight binding to fit all round four sides of the quilt cover. Press open, lay piping cord on WS of straight binding. Fold straight binding over the cord matching edges. Enclose neatly and stitch along piping cord edge either by hand or by machine. See page 113 for further details.

(Pattern continued on page 132)

STOP THE PRESS!
Always press fabrics lightly before quilting as ironing afterwards will tend to flatten the wadding. One method is to pin out the knitted fabric as taut as possible, press with a damp cloth and leave pinned out to 'dry' before design marking.

HOW TO QUILT

          a   b   c

This simple knitted cushion cover emulates the whitework found in the 1820s in the British Isle. The decoration is appliqué, with a white cotton plaited flower corsage and flower motifs in needle lace.

Whitework cushion

THE ESSENTIALS

Measurements

30 x 40cm (12 x 16in)

Materials

Rowan *Cotton 4-ply,* 50g/1¾ ball, approx 170m/185yd (cotton)
    10 x Bleached

3.25mm (US 3) needles

140cm (56in) binding (see page 112)

140cm (56in) Mountmellick Fringe (see page 124)

4 tassels (see page 128)

12 flower embellishments (see page 126)

30 x 40cm (12 x 16in) cushion pad

4 buttons (optional)

Tension

27–29 sts and 28 rows to 10cm (4in) over St st using 3.00mm (US 2–3) needles.

Note

You may need more yarn, depending on the size of your cushion pad and the size and number of embellishments added from the gallery.

Stitches used

Stocking Stitch
Reverse Stocking Stitch
Garter Stitch (binding)

Abbreviations

See page 136.

Cushion

Pattern is in multiples of 24sts.
Cast on 204 sts.
Knit first row.
Row 1: *K12, p12, k12, p12; rep from * to end of row.
Row 2: *P12, k12, p12, k12; rep from * to end of row.
Rows 3–16: Rep last two rows seven times more.
Row 17: *P12, k12, p12, k12; rep from * to end of row.
Row 18: *K12, p12, k12, p12; rep from * to end of row.
Rows 19–32: Rep last two rows seven times more.
These 32 rows form the pattern.
Continue until length of cushion cover required has been reached.
Cast (bind) off.

Making up

Press fabric carefully. Fold so that opening is at the centre back of the cushion. Enclose these opening edges at centre back with lengths of knitted binding. To create binding, cast on 8 sts and garter stitch to the length of the cushion. Make two in total, sew as you would for piping on each edge of the cushion.

Now with wrong sides together, pin and sew front to back, ensuring you have a 2.5cm (1in) overlap on back panels. Use either buttons with loops or knitted I-cord for ties to close.

Embellishments

Stitch the knitted binding into place all around the four sides of the cushion, then slip stitch the Mountmellick fringe into place. Add a tassel at each corner, then add the required number of flower embellishments.

ADORNMENT

Make all the flower decorations in one go. Hold in place with pins before sewing and securing to cushion cover so their position can be changed around until you are completely happy, without defacing the knitting. The cushion has piping and Mountmellick fringe, which are traditional for this type of whitework, but you can choose alternative embellishments (see page 110).

Families linked to the fishing industry around the British coast traditionally produced their own localized patterns of knitting stitches. This rug is based on the textile practices around Filey in Yorkshire during the 19th century.

Vintage floor rug

THE ESSENTIALS

Measurements
Approx 75cm x 105cm (30 x 42in)

Materials
Rowan *4-ply Cotton*, 50g/1¾oz balls, approx 185yd/170m (cotton)
 9 x Bleached (A)
Rowan *Cotton Glacé*, 50g/1¾oz balls, approx 115m/125yd (cotton)
 9 x Bleached (B)
Rowan *Cotton Tape*, 50g/1¾oz balls, approx 65m/72yd (cotton)
 2 x Bleached (C)
3.75mm (US 5) needles
3.75mm (US 5) circular needle
Pair of 3.25mm (US 3) double-pointed needles
Tapestry needle

Tension
Tension should be according to the manufacturers recommendations; however, my preference is for a tight tension to give the rug a more robust feel so I use a needle size from 3.75mm (US 5) upwards.

Note
All yarn amounts are dependant on size of rug knitted.

Stitches used
Reverse Stocking Stitch
Stocking Stitch
Moss Stitch doubled

Abbreviations
See page 136.

Rug base
Using A and 3.75mm (US 5) needles, cast on 160 sts.
Rows 1–8: Reverse St st.
Row 9: With RS facing, * p1, k18, p1; rep from * to end of row.
Row 10: *K1, p18, k1; rep from * to end of row.
Row 11: *K1, p2, k14, p2, k1; rep from * to end of row.
Row 12: *P1, k2, p14, k2, p1; rep from * to end of row.
Row 13: *P1, k2, p2, k10, p2, k2, p1; rep from * to end of row.
Row 14: *K1, p2, k2, p10, k2, p2, k1; rep from * to end of row.
Row 15: *K1, p2, k2, p2, k6, p2, k2, p2, k1; rep from * to end of row.
Row 16: *P1, k2, p2, k2, p6, k2, p2, k2, p1; rep from * to end of row.
Row 17: *P1, k2, p2, k2, p2, k2, p2, k2, p2, k2, p1; rep from * to end of row.
Row 18: *K1, p2, k2, p2, k2, p2, k2, p2, k2, p2, k1; rep from * to end of row.
Rows 19–20: Rep rows 15–16.
Rows 21–22: Rep rows 13–14.
Rows 23–24: Rep rows 11–12.
Rows 25–26: Rep rows 9–10.
Rows 1–26 make up the main pattern and should be repeated as many times as necessary to reach the length of rug required. In the sample in the photograph, 17 times more.
When this is reached, rep rows 1–8 once more to finish.
Cast (bind) off.

Long edge of rug
Using the circular needles as a normal straight pair, pick up multiples of 20 sts along the longest side. For the rug in the photograph, 260 sts. Knitting back and forth, repeat main patt rows 1–26 once, then rows 1–8 once only.
Cast (Bind) off.

Repeat this on the other long edge. Press the edges carefully and hem. Turn under reverse St st rows 1–8 and slip stitch into place and press. This provides the base for the looped knitting. Repeat for all other sides.

Braided cords
(see Embellishments, page 112)
Attach the braids approx 5cm (2in) inside the outer edge of rug. Begin and end at a corner. For the braids, make three I-Cords, each measuring 3.6m (4yd) in length. Adjust length accordingly if size of rug is different from above. Sew into position to main body of rug beginning and ending at one corner.

Fur fringe
(see Embellishments, page 124)
Using B, create enough looped knitting to edge all four sides. Sew to outer edges.

Daisy (make 4)
(see Embellishments, page 128)
Sew firmly to secure, one for each corner. Use one to cover the start and finish of the braid already inserted.

This detailed bedcover is made up of panels of tumbling pointed leaves. The border pattern can be traced back to the 18th century and is sometimes known as 'godmother's lace'. This counterpane works just as well in fine cotton.

Lacy leaf throw

THE ESSENTIALS

Measurements
Approx 210 x 165cm (84 x 66in)

Materials
Louet *Euroflax Paris*, 100g/3½oz cones (linen), approx 523m/570yd

    10 x Pure White

3.25mm (US 3) needles

Tapestry needle

Tension
32sts and 40 rows to 10cm (4 in) over St st using 3.25mm (US 3) needles.

Note
This bedspread is made up of five panels, 2½ repeats wide, plus an edge approx 25cm (10in) in width.

Four open work insertions are needed. Make each insertion 1 full repeat wide and ADD an edge approx 2.5cm (1in) wide to all sides.

Make an edge approx 2.5cm (1in) in width for each side edge of completed bed cover.

A Godmother's Lace border is added to each side of finished blanket, each one approx 15cm (6in) in width.

The pattern given here for the Godmother's Lace borders includes the open work insertion, to save knitting these separately.

Stitches used
Tumbling Leaf
Openwork
Godmother's Lace

Abbreviations
See page 136.

Tumbling Leaf
Pattern is in multiples of 12+2 sts.
Row 1: *P2, yo, k1, yo, p2, k2, k2tog, k3; rep from * to end.
Row 2: *K2, p6, k2, p3; rep from * to end, k2.
Row 3: *P2, [k1, yo] x2, k1, p2, k2, k2tog, k2; rep from * to end, p2
Row 4: *K2, p5; rep from * to end, k2.
Row 5: *P2, k2, yo, k1, yo, k2, p2, k2, k2tog, k1; rep from * to end, p2.
Row 6: *K2, p4, k2, p7; rep from * to end, k2.
Row 7: *P2, k3, yo, k1, yo, k3, p2, k2, k2tog; rep from * to end, p2.
Row 8: *K2, p3, k2, p9; rep from * to end, k2.
Row 9: *P2, k2, k2tog, k5, p2, k1, k2tog; rep from * to end, p2.
Row 10: *K2, p2, k2, p8; rep from * to end, k2.
Row 11: *P2, k2, k2tog, k4, p2, k2tog; rep from * to end, p2.
Row 12: *K2, p1, k2, p7; rep from * to end, k2.
Row 13: *P2, k2, k2tog, k3, p2, yo, k1, yo; rep from * to end, p2.
Row 14: *K2, p3, k2, p6; rep from * to end, k2.
Row 15: *P2, k2, k2tog, k2, p2, [k1, yo] x2, k1; rep from * to end, p2.
Row 16: *K2, p5; rep from * to end, k2.
Row 17: *P2, k2, k2tog, k1, p2, k2, yo, k1, yo, k2; rep from * to end, p2.
Row 18: *K2, p7, k2, p4; rep from * to end, k2.
Row 19: *P2, k2, k2tog, p2, k3, yo, k1, yo, k3; rep from * to end, p2.
Row 20: *K2, p9, k2, p3; rep from * to end, k2.
Row 21: *P2, k1, k2tog, p2, k2, k2tog, k5; rep from * to end, p2.
Row 22: *K2, p8, k2, p2; rep from * to end, k2.
Row 23: *P2, k2tog, p2, k2, k2tog, k4; rep from * to end, p2
Row 24: *K2, p7, k2, p1; rep from * to end, k2.
Starting with row 1, rep these 24 rows until desired length is reached.

Openwork insertion panel
(For five leaf panels make four insertions, to edge completed bedcover, four more)
Pattern is in multiples of 6+2 sts.
Row 1: *P2, k2tog, yo twice, k2tog tbl; rep from * to end, p2.
Row 2: K2, *p1, work 2 sts into yo from preceding row [k1, p1,] p1, k2; rep from * to end.
Row 3: *P2, k4; rep from * to end, p2.
Row 4: K2, *p1, k1, p2, k2; rep from * to end.
These 4 rows form the pattern.

Godmother's Lace border
(Make four, one for each outside edge. For convenience this pattern includes the open work insertion)
Cast on 26 sts.
Knit 1 row.
Row 1: Sl1, p1, k2tog, yo twice, k2tog, tbl, k2, [yfwd, k2tog] 8 times, yo, k2.
Row 2: Knit to last 6 sts. p1, [k1,p1] into previous yo twice, p1, k2.
Row 3: Sl1, p1, k9, [yo, k2tog,] 7 times, yo, k2.

(Pattern continued on page 132)

Bolsters were very popular with the Victorians; the more sumptuous the better. They could be of silk, velvet, or even cotton. The Chevron Pattern offers plenty of texture, and the embellishments add a decorative touch.

Lace and eyelet bolster

Measurements

45cm long x 17cm in diameter (18 x 6¾in)

Materials

Yeoman Yarns *Brittany Cotton*, 450g/16oz cones, approx 2150m/1950yd (cotton)

    2 cones x white

3.75mm (US 5) needles

165cm (66in) of 2.5cm (1in) wide garter stitch band

2 x 165cm (66in) of I-cord to braid for bolster ends

4 x 107cm (43in) lengths of I-cord for scroll embellishment (see pages 127)

Bolster cushion pad

2 short tassels (see page 126)

20–30cm x 15cm (8–12in x 6in) lengths of 2.5cm (1in) garter stitch band for fastening

4–6 rings

Tapestry needle

Tension

23sts and 35 rows to 10cm (4in) over St st using 3.75mm (US 5) needles.

Stitches used

Chevron
Stocking Stitch
Garter Stitch

Abbreviations

See page 136.

Chevron pattern

Pattern is in multiples of 20+3 sts
Using 3 strands of 2-ply [one from each cone] cast on 123 sts.
Knit one row.
Row 1: K1, p5, [k2tog, k3, yo, k1, yo, k3, k2tog tbl, p9] 5 times, k2tog, k3, yo, k1, yo, k3, k2tog, tbl, p5, k1.
Row 2 and all even rows: Knit all k sts. Purl all p sts.
Row 3: K1, p4, [k2tog, k3, yo, k3, yo, k3, k2tog tbl, p7] 5 times, k2tog, k3, yo, k3, yo, k3, k2tog, tbl, p4, k1.
Row 5: K1, p3, [k2tog, k3, yo, k5, yo, k3, k2tog, tbl, p5] 5 times, k2tog, k3, yo, k5, yo, k3, k2tog, tbl, p3, k1.
Row 7: K1, p2, [k2tog, k3, yo, k7, yo, k3, k2tog, tbl, p3] 5 times, k2tog, k3, yo, k7, yo, k3, k2tog, p2, k1.
Row 9: K1, p1, [k2tog, k3, yo, k9, yo, k3, k2tog, tbl, p1] 5 times, k2tog, k3, yo, k9, yo, k3, k2tog, tbl, p1, k1.
Repeat pattern until the desired length has been reached.
(Approx 60cm/24in for circumference of bolster plus extra for overlap).
Cast (bind) off.

Making up

Follow step-by-step instructions and diagrams to make up bolster.

1 Block and press the chevron knitting. See diagram a.

2 Place the 165cm (66in) length of garter stitch band approx 5cm (2in) along three sides of the bolster omitting the curved chevron edge. Sew into place down the centre of the garter stitch band. See diagram b.

3 Braid two 165cm (66in) lengths of I-cord. Place the I-cord on top of the garter stitch band and slipstitch braid into place. See diagram c. Allow braid embellishment to follow the chevron curve at bolster opening. Do not apply braid the embellishment at the top end opposite bolster opening.

4 Use approx 107cm (43in) of I-cord for each scroll shape. Stitch each scroll to the body of fabric.

5 Prepare and pleat both sides of bolster edge and stitch down pleats. See diagram d. Now wrap bolster case around bolster cushion, matching sides. Pin sides matching circle edges and allowing a slight overlap for opening.

6 The pleated circle ends will leave an exposed opening. Cover this with a braided I-cord by spiralling as seen in photograph.

7 Attach a tassel at the centre of each end. Close the side of the bolster with buttons and loops, or with rings and straps. Make 3 or 4 closures, depending on length of bolster. Each closure needs 2 rings. Fold one 15 cm (6 in) length of 2.5cm (1in) wide garter stitch band through 2 rings and stitch the ends under one edge of the opening. Repeat for each fastening. See diagram e.

8 Stitch down one end of another strip of garter stitch band to the other side of the opening. Thread the strap through the two rings and tighten to fasten. Repeat for each fastening.

MAKING UP A BOLSTER

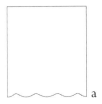
a

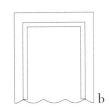
b

c

d

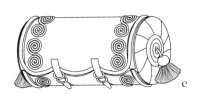
e

Knitted curtains and lampshade covers were extremely popular in the 19th century and still look good today. The panel, tieback and lampshade are also decorated with ringwork flowers, which are simple and easy to make.

Lace and flower décor

THE ESSENTIALS

Measurements

Lace Café Panel: 112 x 65cm (45 x 26in)

Lampshade: height 15cm (6in); diameter at top 12.5cm (5in); diameter at base 22.5cm (9in) approx.

Materials

Louet *Euroflax Paris*, 100g/3½oz balls (linen), approx 523m/570yd

1 x Pure White

8.00mm (US 11) needles

3.25mm (US 3) needles

Ringwork flower embellishments (see page 128)

Plain lampshade

Tapestry needle

Tension

12sts and 20 rows to 10cm (4in) over St st using 8.00mm (US 11) needles.

Note

Large and small flowers can be made up and sewn together to make up a rosette. It is fascinating how one pattern can look totally different when knitted on a larger needle, or the pattern is repeated differently to obtain a special effect.

The lampshade cover is not designed to replace a lampshade, only to be used for decorative purposes. Either cover a store-bought lampshade, as here, or make up your own lampshade.

Stitches used

Openwork
Lily pattern

Abbreviations

See page 136.

Openwork insertion pattern

Pattern is in multiples of 6+2 sts.
Row 1: *P2, k2tog, yo twice, k2tog tbl; rep from * to last two sts, p2.
Row 2: *K2, p1, [k1, p1] into each yo from previous row, p1; rep from * to two last sts, k2.
Row 3: *P2, k4; rep from * to last two sts, p2.
Row 4: *K2, p1, k1, p1, k1; rep from * to last two sts, k2.
These 4 rows form the pattern.
Rep these 4 rows to required length.

Lace café panel

This panel gives privacy without cutting out too much light to any room. The yarn allows starching as well as having good 'hanging' qualities.

Using 8.00mm (US 11) needles, cast on 98 sts. Work open work insertion panel pattern for 50 rep.
Cast (bind) off.

Making up

Make as many ringwork flowers as desired and stitch onto the panel with matching thread.

Flowered tie back panel

This beautiful pattern can either be left as it is, starched, or covered in needle flowers – as shown in the photograph – for added weight.

Lily pattern

Using 3.25mm (US 3) needles, cast on 19 sts. Knit one row.
Row 1 and every WS row except 5 and 13: [WS] Purl.
Row 2: K2, yo, k2 tog, yo, [k2tog] 3 times, k2, yo, k3, yo, ssk, yo, k2. (19 sts)
Row 4: K2, yo, k2 tog, [k3 tog] twice, yo, k1, yo, k2, [ssk, yo] twice, k2. (17 sts)

(Pattern continued on page 132)

LACE FLOWERS

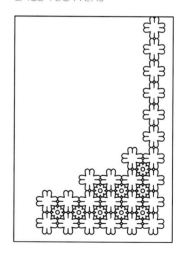

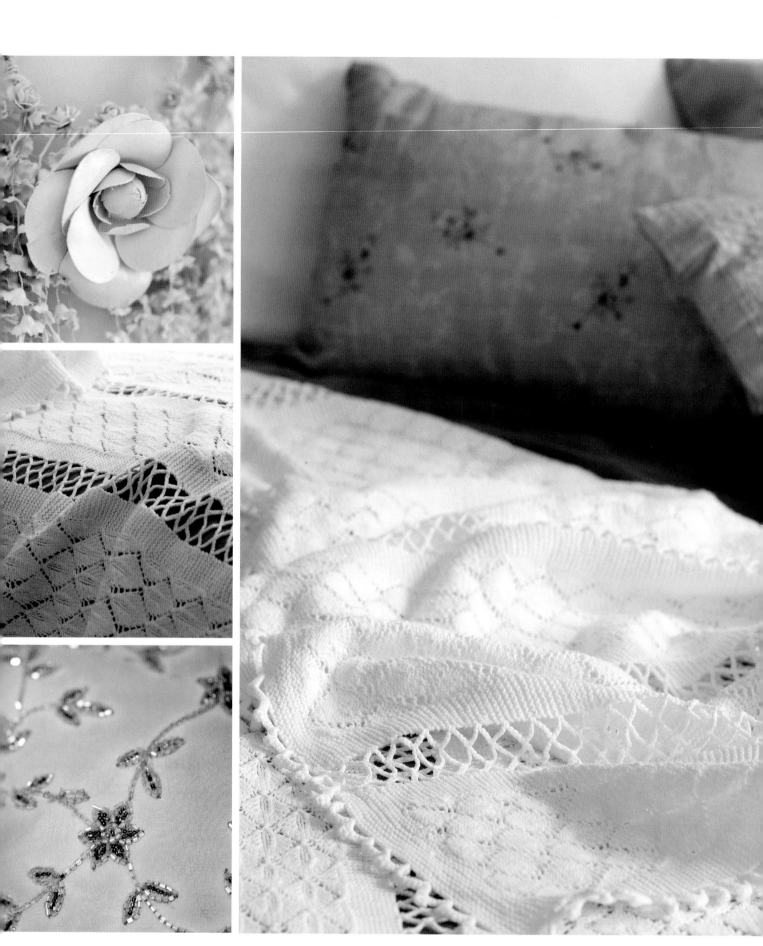

The materials and pattern used in this throw are based on a century-old crib cover. Each panel border and insertion is crocheted in honeycomb. The yarn used seeks to replicate that which would have been common at the time.

Honeycomb throw

THE ESSENTIALS

Measurements
Each panel: 20 x 155cm (8 x 62in)
Finished throw: 140 x 155cm (56 x 62in)

Materials
Yeoman Yarns *Brittany 2-ply*, 450g/16oz, approx 2150m/1950yd (cotton)
 2 cones x White for
 Summer version
 OR
Yeoman Yarns *Cotton Club 4-ply*, 450g/16oz, approx 1800m/1650yd (cotton)
 2 cones x White for
 Winter version
2.75–3.25mm (US 2–3) needles
3.25–3.75mm (D/3–F/5) crochet hook

Tension
The tension for this project is not critical.

Stitches used
Garter Stitch
Old Open Leaf Stitch

Note
There are 7 panels for the throw, which are made separately and crocheted together at the end.

The pattern for these panels is worked in multiples of 14+1 sts. A further 14 sts should be added for the garter st border, 7 sts on either side of the panel.

Abbreviations
See page 136.

Old Open Leaf panel
Cast on 57 sts, knit 14 rows then work as follows:
Row 1: K7, [k1, k2tog, k4, yo, k1, yo, k4, k2tog tbl] three times, k1, k7.
Rows 2, 4, 6, 8, 10: K7, purl to last 7 sts, k7.
Row 3: K7, [k1, k2tog, k3, yo twice, k3, k2togtbl] three times, k1, k7.
Row 5: K7, [k1, k2tog, k2, yo, k5, yo, k2, k2tog tbl] three times, p1, k7.
Row 7: K7, [k1, k2tog, k1, yo, k7, yo, k1, k2togtbl] three times, p1, k7.
Row 9: K7, [k1, k2tog, yo, k9, yo, k2togtbl] k1, k7.
Row 11: K7, k2togtbl, [yo, k11, yo, sl1, k2tog, psso,] twice, yo, k11, yo, k2tog, k7.
Row 12: K7, purl to last 7 stitches, k7.
Row 13: K7, [k1, yo, k4, k2togtbl, k1, k2tog, k4, yo] three times k1, k7.
Rows 14, 16, 18, 20, 22: K7, p to last 7 sts.
Row 15: K7, k2, [yo, k3, k2togtbl, k1, k2tog, k3, yo, k3] twice, yo, k3, k2togtbl, k1, k2tog, k3, yo, k2, k7.
Row 17: K7, k3, [yo, k2, k2togtbl, k1, k2tog, k2, yo, k5] twice, yo, k2, k2togtbl, k1, k2tog, k2, yo, k3, k7.
Row 19: K7, k4, [yo, k1, k2togtbl, k1, k2tog, k1, yo, k7] twice, yo, k1, k2togtbl, k1, k2tog, k1, yo, k4, k7.
Row 21: K7, k5, [yo, k2togtbl, k1, k2tog, yo, k9] twice, yo, k2togtbl, k1, k2tog, yo, k5, k7.
Row 23: K7, k6, [yo, sl1, k2tog, psso, yo, k11] twice, yo, sl1, k2tog, psso, yo, k11, k6, k7.
Row 24: K7, purl to last 7 sts, k7.
These 24 rows form the pattern.
Repeat these rows until the desired

length is reached.
Knit 14 rows.
Cast (bind) off.

Making up
Make the number of panels for the desired width – the throw in the photograph has 7 panels across. Pin out and press all panels ready to receive the insertion and border of your choice.

Joining panels
Crochet a honeycomb filling pattern to link each panel as follows:
Pattern is in multiples of 4+1 chain plus 5 extra turning chains, so make 30 ch.
Row 1: 1dc into 10th ch from the hook, *6ch, miss 3ch, 1dc into next ch; rep. from * to end, turn.
Row 2: 9ch, 1dc into the first 6ch sp of previous row, *6ch, 1dc into next 6ch sp; rep from * to end, working last dc into first 9ch sp, turn.
The second row forms the pattern.

Chain stitch a single row for the outside edge.

MIX AND MATCH
Try making this throw using the Openwork insertion panel used for Lacy Leaf Throw on page 44, or choose another alternative panel design such as the flowered tie back on page 52 without the flowers.

1960

Candlewick squares were used to make counterpanes during America's pioneering days. This cushion uses the same idea, but with one square. The candlewick stitch used is the French Knot and the lacy edging is the picot point.

Candlewick cushion

Measurements

30 x 37.7cm (12 x 15in)

Materials

Andru Knitwear *Italian Silk*, 25g/⅞oz cone

    4 x Mauve 928

12.75mm (US 17) needles

30 x 37.5cm (12 x 15in) cushion pad with a cream fabric cover suitable for embroidery

Tapestry ring (optional)

Tapestry needle

Tension

Tension is not really important on this project – the lace can be knitted as loose or as tight as preferred.

Note

If you cannot find a suitable cushion, you can make your own cover from plain cream fabric to embroider.

If you do not want a freeform design, such as the one used here, an embroidery transfer design will work equally well.

See instructions for French Knot on page 133.

Abbreviations

See page 136.

Special abbreviation

Picot = Make Picot as follows: for each picot cast on 2 sts, knit these two sts, pass first st over 2nd, knit one more st, pass first st over 2nd st again, leaving one loop on needle.

Picot point lace edging

Using 12.75mm (US 17) needles, cast on 15 sts.
Knit one row, then work as follows:
Row 1: Sl1, k1, yo, p2tog, k3, yo twice, k2tog, k6.
Row 2: Picot, k7, p1, k3, yo, p2tog, k2.
Row 3: Sl1, k1, yo, p2tog, k5, yo twice, k2tog, k5.
Row 4: Picot, k6, p1, k5, yo, p2tog, k2.
Row 5: Sl1, k1, yo, p2tog, k7, yo twice, k2tog, k4.
Row 6: Picot, k5, p1, k7, yo, p2tog, k2.
Row 7: Sl1, k1, yo, p2tog, k9, yo twice, k2tog, k3.
Row 8: Picot, k4, p1, k9, yo, p2tog, k2.
Row 9: Sl1, k1, yo, p2tog, k11, yo twice, k2tog, k2.
Row 10: Picot, k3, p1, k11,yo, p2tog, k2.
Row 11: Sl1, k1, yo, p2tog, k13, yo twice, k2tog, k1.
Row 12: Picot, k2, p1, k13, yo, p2tog, k2.
Row 13: Sl1, k1, yo, p2tog, k15, yo twice, k2tog.
Row 14: Picot, k1, p1, k15, yo, p2tog, k2.
Row 15: Sl1, k1, yo, p2tog, k18.
Row 16: *Cast on two sts, k4, pass 3 sts over first one after each other. Place remaining st back onto left hand needle and repeat from * six times more, then leaving last loop on right needle, k10, yo, p2tog, k2. Repeat last 16 rows for length required.

Shape lace corner

Row 1: Sl1, k1, yo, p2tog, k3, yo twice, k2tog, k6
Row 2: Picot, k7, p1, k3, leave 4 sts unworked and turn.
Row 3: Sl1, k4, yo twice, k2tog, k5.
Row 4: Picot, k6, p1, k4, leave 5 sts unworked and turn.
Row 5: Sl1, k5, yo twice k2tog, k4.
Row 6: Picot, k5, p1, k5, leave 6 sts unworked and turn.
Row 7: Sl1, k6, yo twice, k2tog, k3.
Row 8: Picot, k4, p1, k6, leave 7 sts unworked and turn.
Row 9: Sl1, k7, yo twice, k2tog, k2.
Row 10: Picot, k3, p1, k7, leave 8 sts unworked and turn.
Row 11: Sl1, k8, yo twice, k2tog, k1.
Row 12: Picot, k2, p1, k8, leave 9 sts unworked and turn.
Row 13: Sl1, k9, yo twice, k2tog.
Row 14: Picot, k1, p1, k9, leave 10 sts unworked and turn.
Row 15: Sl1, k11.
Row 16: Cast on 2, k4, pass three sts over first st, place this st onto left hand needle as before, k10, yo, p2tog, k2. Continue with straight lace from row 1. Cast (bind) off.

Making up

Once length is complete, press lightly and slip stitch into place on cushion cover.

(**Pattern continued on page 133**)

This cushion design contains both traditional and modern elements and uses woven garter stitch strips to emphasize this. It expands the perception of knitting as a craft and is sure to tempt both the beginner and the expert.

Basketweave cushion

THE ESSENTIALS

Measurements

50 x 50cm (20 x 20in)

Materials

Louet *Euroflax Paris,* 100g/3½oz cone, approx 530m/580yd (wool)

3 cones x Pure White

50cm (20in) square cushion pad

2.25–3.00mm (US 1–2) needles

2 pieces of cream sateen each approx 50 x 50cm (20 x 20in) for cushion pad

40cm (16in) cream zip (optional)

200cm (80in) piping for cushion sides (optional)

Pins

Stapler

Tension

Tension is not critical on this project, but select a needle size to give a fairly firm, close-knit fabric.

Note

Each knitted strip is made 45cm (18in) long and stretched slightly to 50cm (20in) to give tautness to the finished fabric.

The cushion pad needs to be slightly too large for the cover to bring out the pattern of the woven strips.

Stitches used

Garter Stitch

Abbreviations

See page 136.

Knitted strips

Cast on 12 sts.

Row 1: Knit to last st, knit into back of last st – this gives more definition to the outside edge.

Repeat this row until strip measures 45cm (18in).

Cast (bind) off.

Make 40 strips.

Making up

Pin out one piece of cream fabric as tautly as possible – it should not be moved until all strips of knitting have been woven.

Lay each knitted strip out closely together.

Beginning at one side edge of the pinned out material, staple one end of a strip to the cream fabric as close to the bottom edge as possible. Pull gently on the other end of the strip to stretch it to the opposite side of the fabric and staple this end close to the edge. Repeat with the first 20 strips, so the fabric is covered in a layer of vertical knitted strips set closely next to each other.

Using one of the remaining 20 strips, lay it horizontally along the bottom edge of the fabric and staple one end only, close to one side edge of the fabric. Carefully weave the strip under and over the fixed strips and pin at the other end to hold in place. Repeat with the next strip, taking it over where the first went under and vice versa, to build up a weaving pattern. Repeat with each of the remaining strips. Once the weaving is completed, make sure that all the strips are parallel and in straight lines then staple the pinned ends and remove the pins. Avoiding the staples, hand or machine stitch across the end of every strip around 6mm (¼in) in from the edge.

Make up the cushion cover in the normal way, using the other piece of fabric as the backing and inserting the zip and piping if required. Remove the staples at the end.

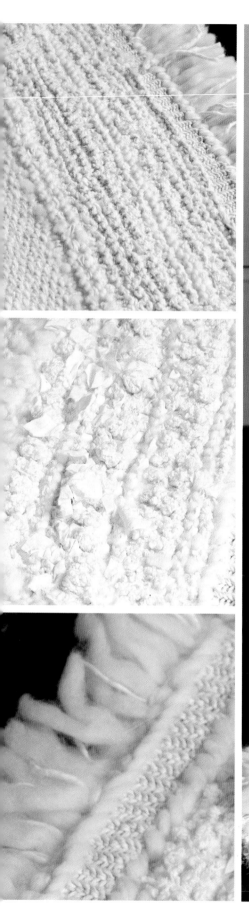

Knitted rugs have had a revival recently and for a beginner knitter, it's a marvellous way to learn the craft. Not only are they practical, they are fashionably shabby chic and inexpensive to make using leftover yarns and fabrics.

Rag rug sampler

THE ESSENTIALS

Measurements

50 x 80cm (20 x 32in) including fringe

Materials

Strong cotton yarn

Rowan *All Seasons Cotton*, 50g/1¾oz balls, approx 160m/175yd (cotton blend)

2 x Organic (A)

Rowan *Biggy Print,* 100g/3½oz balls, approx 30m/33yd (wool)

2 x Sheep (B)

Rowan *Big Wool Tuft*, 50g/1¾oz balls, approx 25m/27yd (wool)

2 x White Hot

Lengths of cream-coloured cloth (e.g. torn up sheeting)

6.00mm (US 10) needles

10.00mm (US 15) needles (optional)

15.00mm (US 19) needles (optional)

Four tassels (See page 126.)

Tension

This is dependant on types of yarn being used – the thicker the better for most rugs. 7.5 sts and 10 rows to 10cm (4in) over St st using 15.00mm (US 19) needles, 9 sts and 12 rows to 10cm (4in) over St st using 10.00mm (US 15) needles.

Stitches used

Rug Stitch

Linen Stitch

Moss or Rice Stitch

Knitweaving

Abbreviations

See page 136.

Notes

Rugs can be knitted in the normal way – only the evenness and the firmness of your work will affect the finished item. Experiment to find the texture you like best.

Using the same yarn thickness throughout overcomes any difficulties with the tension and having to alter needle size. Combine several yarns together or try using fabric and yarn together.

Rug Stitch (A)

This stitch is used for adding strips of fabric to your rug.

Cast on required number of stitches.

Row 1: Knit.

Row 2 (WS): K1, *place a strip of fabric or yarn across at right angles to the knitting between needles with most of the length on RS of work and knit next stitch. Bring the long end of strip back to WS and holding it over the tip of the left hand needle k1. The fabric strip is now secured in the knitting*. K1, rep from * to *, k1. Rep to end of row, replacing strips of fabric as necessary.

Row 3: Rep row 2 but stagger the position of the fabric strips.

Woven stitches

These patterns give a fabric effect. The stitches create a firm texture and patterns of not more than two rows have been chosen. Since the woven stitches cause the fabric to become denser, choose a larger needle to avoid the stitches pulling in and narrowing the width of your rug.

Linen Stitch (B)

Pattern is worked in multiples of 2 sts.

Row 1: *K1, yarn forward, sl1 purlwise, yarn back; rep from * to end.

Row 2: *P1, yarn back, sl1, purlwise, yarn forward; rep from * to end.

Rep these two rows.

Twice knit knitting (C)

Both versions can be seen in Embellishments (see page 110).

Moss or Rice Stitch (D)

Worked in multiples of 2 sts.

Row 1: *K1, p1; rep from * to end.

Row 2: *P1, k1; rep from * to end.

Rep these two rows.

Knitweaving

A second yarn is woven into the fabric, without knitting any stitches with it. It acts like a float, as the yarn is woven in and out between sts. It is useful for ends of yarn nothing can be done with.

Rug

Using 6.00mm (US 10) needles and All Seasons cotton, cast on approx 120 sts. Vary the pattern by working the following:

Knit 2.5cm (1in) of pattern C.

Knit 5cm (2in) of pattern A, using Big Wool Tuft. Knit in scraps of linen/ sheeting at random intervals.

Using one pair US 15 (10.00mm) needles and All Seasons, knit 2.5cm (1in) of pattern B.

(**Pattern continued on page 133**)

Classic baby blanket

This beautifully nostalgic piece is reminiscent of the handmade covers used in the 1930s. Now you can re-create one to pass on from generation to generation.

THE ESSENTIALS

Measurements

50 x 80cm (20 x 32in) before edging

Materials

Yeoman Yarns *Brittany Cotton 2-ply*, 450g/16oz cones, approx 3800m/4142yd (cotton)

   3 cones in Petal

3.75mm (US 5) needles

3.25mm (US 3) needles

2.75–3.50mm (US 2–4) circular needle

Ringwork flowers (see page 126)

Tension

30–32 sts and 22–24 rows to 10cm (4in) over St st using 3.75mm (US 5) needles.

Note

Because the pattern is based on the triangle, there are several ways of putting the shapes together; either as a square, an octagon, a diamond, or a zigzag.

Stitches used

Garter Stitch
Stocking Stitch
Reverse Stocking Stitch

Abbreviations

See page 136.

Triangle

Using three strands of yarn, one from each cone, and 3.75mm (US 5) needles, cast on 3 sts.

Row 1: Yo, k3.
Row 2: Yo, k4.
Row 3: Yo, k5.
Row 4: Yo, k6.
Row 5: Yo, k7.
Row 6: Yo, k2tog, k2, yo, k4.
Row 7: Yo, k2tog, k2, p1, k4.
Row 8: Yo, k2tog, k2, yo, k1, yo, k4.
Row 9: Yo, k2tog, k2, p3, k4.
Row 10: Yo, k2tog, k2, yo, k3, yo, k4.
Row 11: Yo, k2tog, k2, p5, k4.
Row 12: Yo, k2tog, k2, yo, k5, yo, k4.
Row 13: Yo, k2tog, k2, p7, k4.
Row 14: Yo, k2tog, k2, yo, k7, yo, k4.

Continue to increase in this manner until 35 sts are on needle, ending with RS row.

Next row (WS): Yo, k2tog, k to end of row. (35 sts)
Next row: Yo, k2tog, k2, yo, p27, yo, k4.
Next row: Yo, k2tog, k to end of row.
Next row: Yo, k2tog, k2, yo, k29, yo, k4.
Next row: Yo, k2tog, k2, p31, k4.
Next row: Yo, k2tog, k2, [yo, k2tog] 15 times, k1, yo, k4.
Next row: Yo, k2tog, k to end of row.
Next row: Yo, k2tog, k2, yo, p32, yo, k4.
Next row: Yo, k2tog, k to end of row.
Next row: Yo, k2tog, k2, yo, k34, yo, k4.
Next row: Yo, k2tog, k2, p36, k4
Next row: Yo, k2tog, k2 [yo, k2tog] x 18, yo, k4.
Next row: Yo, k2tog, k to end of row.

Next row: Yo, k2tog, k2, yo, p37, yo, k4.
Next row: Yo, k2tog, k to end of row. Cast (bind) off.

Making up

Make as many triangles as needed to create the desired size. Press each piece lightly. Overlap the garter st edges and stitch through each yo loop with a back-stitch to strengthen the seams. Alternatively, use the yo to link each piece to another.

Make edging

With RS facing and using the circular needle and two strands of yarn, pick up stitches evenly around all four sides of blanket.

Round 1: (RS facing) Purl. (Ridge on sample.)
Rounds 2–5: Knit.
Cast (bind) off.

(Pattern continued on page 133)

CRIB NOTES

If you would like to create this for a baby carriage, measure it first and sketch out how you'll place the triangles together, which will give you an idea of how many triangles to make in total.

This unusual coverlet is based on a narrowboat design. The bonding technique is the flat and tied quilting method. 'Flat' because there is no wadding and 'tied' because individual ties are used to join two pieces of fabric together.

Art Deco quilt

Measurements
135 x 195cm (54 x 78in)

Materials
Rowan *Cotton 4-ply*, 50g/1¼oz balls, approx 170m/186yd (cotton)
   60 x Bleached 113

2.75mm (US 2) needles

3.00mm (US 2–3) needles

3.25mm (US 3) needles

137.5 x 197.5cm (55 x 79in) piece of white muslin fabric to line quilt

Approx 42 strips 6–10mm (¼–⅜in) wide and 10cm (4in) long, cut from any lightweight material for quilt ties

Tapestry needle with large eye to thread quilt ties

Tension
Tension is according to preference. Smaller needles will give a tighter knit and a heavier quilt, which would be useful for a winter. Larger needles will give a looser stitch and have the opposite effect. The quilt shown was made with 3.00mm (US 2–3) needles.

Note
The quilt illustrated has 127 full squares and 10 half squares.

Light fabric is suggested for the lining as it is authentic and is easier to quilt.

Traditionally ties are done on the wrong side, but here are knotted on the front to make a feature of them.

Stitches used
Garter Stitch

Abbreviations
See page 136.

Full square
Cast on 43 sts using thumb method.
Work 9 rows in garter st.
Row 10 (WS): K6, p31, k6.
Row 11 and all RS rows: Knit.
Row 12: K6, p31, k6.
Row 14: K6, p31, k6.
Row 16: K6, p5, k21, p5, k6.
Row 18: K6, p5, k21, p5, k6.
Row 20: K6, p5, k21, p5, k6.
Row 22: K6, p5, k21, p5, k6.
Row 24: K6, p5, k5, p11, k5, p5, k6.
Row 26: K6, p5, k5, p11, k5, p5, k6.
Row 28: K6, p5, k5, p11, k5, p5, k6.
Row 30: K6, p5, k5, p11, k5, p5, k6.
Row 32: K6, p5, k5, p11, k5, p5, k6.
Row 34: K6, p5, k5, p11, k5, p5, k6.
Row 36: K6, p5, k21, p5, k6.
Row 38: K6, p5, k21, p5, k6.
Row 40: K6, p5, k21, p5, k6.
Row 42: K6, p5, k21, p5, k6.
Row 44: K6, p31, k6.
Row 46: K6, p31, k6.
Row 48: K6, p31, k6.
Knit 9 rows.
Cast (bind) off.

Half square
Cast on 23 sts (incl allowance for sewing up) using thumb method.
Knit 9 rows ending with an RS row.
Row 10 (WS): K6, p17.
Row 11 and all alt rows: Knit.
Row 12: K6, p17.
Row 14: K6, p17.
Row 16: K6, p5, k12.
Row 18: K6, p5, k12.
Row 20: K6, p5, k12.
Row 22: K6, p5, k12.
Row 24: K6, p5, k5, p7.
Row 26: K6, p5, k5, p7.
Row 28: K6, p5, k5, p7.
Row 30: K6, p5, k5, p7.
Row 32: K6, p5, k5, p7.
Row 34: K6, p5, k5, p7.
Row 36: K6, p5, k12.
Row 38: K6, p5, k12.
Row 40: K6, p5, k12.
Row 42: K6, p5, k12.
Row 44: K6, p17.
Row 46: K6, p17.
Row 48: K6, p17.
Knit 9 rows.
Cast (bind) off.

Making up
Make as many squares and half squares as needed to make up the desired size of counterpane – the half squares are for edges only. Lay squares out staggered as in building bricks and sew together. See diagram.

Turn under a 12mm (½in) hem round all four sides of the muslin lining. Pin the prepared lining very carefully to the back of quilt, making sure that lining is within 5–7.5cm (2–3in) of the edges of quilt. Tack lining into place.

Thread tapestry needle with a strip of quilt tie fabric and use to stitch the two layers together.

Take the strip down through both layers to back of quilt, bring up to surface approx 6mm (¼in) away, then repeat this again. Now tie the ends of the strips together on the RS in a double knot. Rep with each quilt tie.

HALF SQUARE

SQUARE

X QUILT TIE

The garden plot counterpane

Knitted counterpane throws make instant heirlooms. This version of the garden plot keeps the blistered leaf and row of diagonal leaves, but the ridged pattern of garter stitch incorporates the traditional railroad pattern or Quaker effect.

THE ESSENTIALS

Measurements

240 x 280cm (96 x 112in)

Materials

Yeoman Yarns *Brittany 2-ply*, 450g/16oz cones (cotton), approx 3800m/4142yd

4 cones x White 100 (A)

3.25–3.75mm (US 3–5) needles

Tapestry needle or similar blunt-ended needle

Tension

Tension is not critical on this project.

Notes

Four squares make up one motif. For a single bed approximately 120 squares (30 motifs) will be needed, depending on size of bed.

The loops created by the yarn overs make it easy to join the correct stitches when assembling the counterpane. The making up should enhance the pattern itself.

Edgings can be sewn on afterward by hand or machine, or knitted in with the pattern using the 'pickup' technique.

Stitches used

Stocking Stitch
Garter Stitch
Backstitch for quilting

Abbreviations

See page 136.

One Square

Using two strands of 2-ply **together**, cast on 3 sts.
Row 1: Yo, k1, yo, k1, yo, k1.
Row 2: Yo, k1, p3, k2.
Row 3: Yo, k3, yo, k1, yo, k3.
Row 4: Yo, k2, p5, k3.
Row 5: Yo, k5, yo, k1, yo, k5.
Row 6: Yo, k3, p7, k4.
Row 7: Yo, k7, yo, k1, yo, k7.
Row 8: Yo, k4, p9, k5.
Row 9: Yo, k9, yo, k1, yo, k9.
Row 10: Yo, k5, p11, k6. (23 sts)
Row 11: Yo, k6, k2togtbl, k7, k2tog, k6.
Row 12: Yo, k6, p9, k7.
Row 13: Yo, k7, k2togtbl, k5, k2tog, k7.
Row 14: Yo, k7, p7, k8,
Row 15: Yo, k8, k2togtbl, k3, k2tog, k8,
Row 16: Yo, k8, p5, k9.
Row 17: Yo, k9, k2togtbl, k1, k2tog, k9.
Row 18: Yo, k9, p3, k10.
Row 19: Yo, k10, sl 1, k2tog, psso, k10.
Row 20: Yo, knit to end. (22 sts)
Row 21: Yo, knit to end. (23 sts)
Row 22: Yo, p24.
Row 23: Yo, knit. (25 sts)
Row 24: Yo, k26.
Row 25: Yo, p27.
Row 26: Yo, k28.
Row 27–38: Rep rows 21–26, twice more. (41 sts)
Row 39: Yo, knit to end.
Row 40: Yo, purl to end.
Row 41: Yo, p1, yo, k1, yo, p6, [yo, k1, yo, p6] 5 times. (56 sts)
Row 42: Yo, k6, p3, [k6, p3,] 5 times, k2. (57 sts)

Row 43: Yo, p2, [k1, yo, k1, yo, k1, p6] 6 times, p1. (57 sts)
Row 44: Yo, k7, [p5, k6] 5 times, p5, k3. (71 sts)
Row 45: Yo, p3, [k2, yo, k1, yo, k2, p6] 6 times, p2. (84 sts)
Row 46: Yo, k8, [p7, k6] 5 times, p7, k4. (85 sts)
Row 47: Yo, p4, [k2togtbl, k3, k2tog, p6] 6 times, p3. (74 sts)
Row 48: Yo, k9, [p5, k6] 5 times, p5, k5. (75 sts)
Row 49: Yo, p5, [k2togtbl, k1, k2tog, p6] 6 times, p4. (64 sts)
Row 50: Yo, k10, [p3, k6] 6 times. (65 sts)
Row 51: Yo, p6, [sl 1, k2tog, psso, p6] 6 times, p5. (54 sts)
Row 52: Yo, knit to end. (55 sts)
This is the end of leaf panel, start decrease:
Row 53: Yo, k3tog, knit. (54 sts)
Row 54: Yo, k3tog, purl to end. (53 sts)
Row 55: Yo, k3tog, knit to end. (52 sts)
Row 56: Yo, k3tog, knit to end. (51 sts)
Row 57: Yo, k3tog, [yo, k2tog] to end.
Row 58: Yo, k3tog, knit to end. (49 sts)
Rep rows 53–58 decreasing as before, until no stitches remain.
Fasten off.

Making up

Make as many squares as needed. Pin and block each to a square shape and press carefully, especially the yarn overs at edges.

(**Pattern continued on page 134**)

Ruffled cushion

Although a little more unusual these days, this tailored look was very fashionable in the sixties. The pretty chintz ruffle lends a touch of femininity and complements the textured knitted design.

THE ESSENTIALS

Measurements

45 x 45cm (18 x 18in)

Materials

Rowan Yarns *4-ply cotton*, 50g/1¾oz ball, approx 170m/185yd
    20 x Bleached

3.00mm (US 2–3) needles

1.8m (2yd) piping cord

45cm (18in) cushion pad

270cm (108in) chintz fabric for ruffle piping

4 x 45cm (18in) zips (optional)

Tension

27–29sts and 37–39 rows to 10cm (4in) over St st using 3.00mm (US 2–3) needles.

Note

The quantities given will make four average-size seat cushions.

This cushion is suitable for both indoor and outdoor use.

Stitches used

Stocking Stitch
Reverse Stocking Stitch

Abbreviations

See page 136.

Cushion (make 2)

Worked in multiples of 40 sts.

Row 1: K2, p18, k18, p2.
Row 2: Rep row 1.
Row 3: K4, p16, k16, p4.
Row 4: Rep row 3.
Row 5: K6, p14 k14, p6.
Row 6: Rep row 5.
Row 7: K8, p12, k12, p8.
Row 8: Rep row 7.
Row 9: K10, p10, k10, p10.
Row 10: Rep row 9.
Row 11: K12, p8, k8, p12.
Row 12: Rep row 11.
Row 13: K14, p6, k6, p14.
Row 14: Rep row 13.
Row 15: K16, p4, k4, p16.
Row 16: Rep row 15.
Row 17: K18, p2, k2, p18.
Row 18: Rep row 17.
Row 19: P18, k2, p2, k18.
Row 20: Rep row 19.
Row 21: P16, k4, p4, k16.
Row 22: Rep row 21.
Row 23: P14, k6, p6, k14.
Row 24: Rep row 23.
Row 25: P12, k8, p8, k12.

Row 26: Rep row 25.
Row 27: P10, k10, p10, k10.
Row 28: Rep row 27.
Row 29: P8, k12, p12, k8.
Row 30: Rep row 29.
Row 31: P6, k14, p14, k6.
Row 32: Rep row 31.
Row 33: P4, k16, p16, k4.
Row 34: Rep row 33.
Row 35: P2, k18, p18, k2.
Row 36: Rep row 35.

These 36 rows form the pattern; repeat until enough fabric has been knitted for the cushion.

Making up

Create a ruffle by sewing a running stitch along the raw edge of the material chosen, gathering the fabric until it measures 180cm (72in). After having prepared the piping and ruffle, sandwich it between two pieces of your knitted fabric. Sew around three sides of the cushion with a 1.3cm (½in) seam allowance. Insert zip on 4th side or see gallery for alternative closures.

TRY BEFORE YOU BUY

The idea of cutting and sewing a knitted fabric can easily be translated to other items, such as quilts or children's clothing. Before beginning any work, make a sample of the stitch or pattern to be used, as not all of them are suitable.

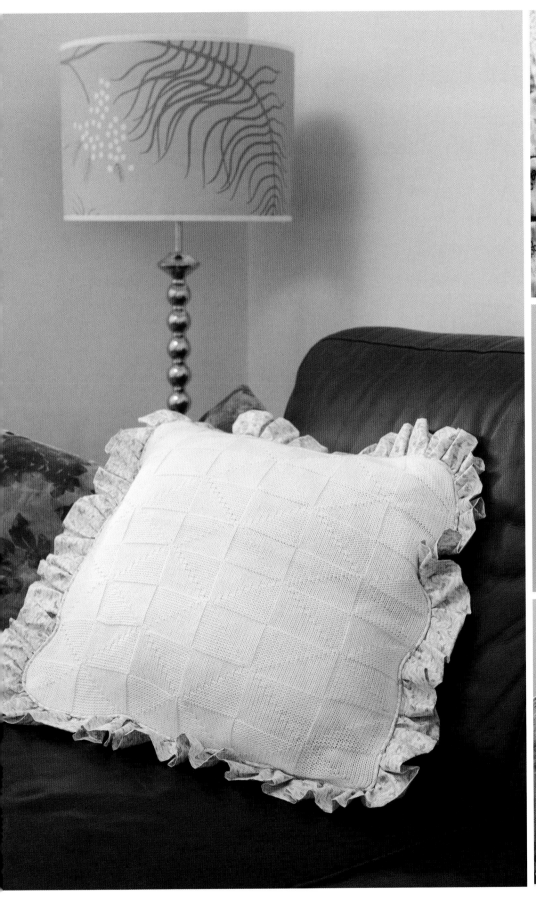

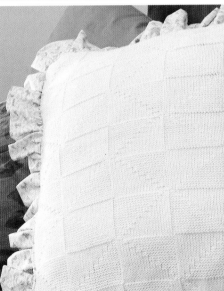

Circular throw

This circular knitted throw was designed because I couldn't find a suitable cover for my granddaughter's circular bed. This is a fun item which is easy and fast to knit. It is ideal for beginners, as it uses the short row technique.

THE ESSENTIALS

Measurements

150cm (60in) in diameter

Materials

Rowan *Big Wool Tuft*, 50g/1¾oz balls, approx 25m/27yd (wool)

    44 x Frost (A)

Rowan *Big Wool*, 100g/3½oz balls, approx 80m/87yd (cotton)

    12 x White Hot (B)

10.00mm (US 15) needles

Tension

9–10sts and 12–14 rows to 10cm (4in) over St st using 10.00mm (US 15) needles.

Note

You can use any yarn for this cover, but will need to follow the tension given.

Stitches used

Garter Stitch

Abbreviations

See page 136.

Special abbreviation

MB = Make bobble as follows: knit into front then back of stitch twice, then into front again. Slip 2nd, 3rd, 4th, and 5th loops over first stitch. Leave on right hand needle making sure bobble stays to front of work (RS).

Throw

Using B, cast on 65 sts.

Knit 1 row.

Row 2 (RS): *K4, MB; rep from * to last five sts, k5. (12 bobbles)

Row 3 (WS): K5, *MB (making sure bobble stays to back of work (RS), k4; rep from * to end of row. Make sure 2nd set of bobbles is immediately above first set. Break off yarn.

Join in A.

Next row: With A, k5, turn.

Next and following alt rows: With yarn at back of work, slip first st off right hand needle onto left hand needle. Bring yarn to front of work and slip the slipped st back onto right hand needle.

When turning always slip first st in this manner to prevent a hole.

Knit to end of row.

Next row: K10, turn.

Next row: K15, turn.

Next row: K20, turn.

Next row: K25, turn.

Continue in this manner, working 5 sts more every alt row until all sts have been worked.

Next row: Knit to end of row. (65 sts) Break off A.*

These 28 rows complete one pattern. Repeat from * to * 28 times in total, alternating B and A, omitting last four rows on the last pattern. (28 double bobbles)

Cast (bind) off.

Centre

Close the throw by sewing two sides together. Close the centre hole with bobble insert.

Cast on 10 stitches with B.

Knit one row then proceed as follows:

Row 1: K2, MB, k1, MB, k1, MB, k1, MB, k1, turn.

Row 2: Knit.

Row 3: K3, MB, k1, MB, k1, MB, k1, turn.

Row 4: Knit.

Row 5: K2, MB, k1, MB, k1, MB, k1, turn.

Row 6: Knit.

Row 7: K3, MB, k1, MB, k1, turn.

Row 8: Knit.

Row 9: K2, MB, k1, MB, k1, turn.

Row 10: Knit.

Row 11: K3, MB, k1, turn.

Row 12: Knit.

Row 13: K2, MB, k1, turn.

Row 14: Knit.

Row 15: Knit to end.

Row 16: Knit to end.

These 16 rows form the short row technique.

Rep these 16 rows until an entire circle of bobbles has been completed.

Cast (bind) off.

Leaves

Using B, cast on 3 sts.

Row 1: K1, yo, k1, yo, k1.

Row 2: Purl.

Row 3: K2, yo, k1, yo, k2.

Row 4: Purl.

Row 5: K3, yo, k1, yo, k3.

Row 6: Purl.

Row 7: K4, yo, k1, yo, k4.

Row 8: Purl.

Row 9: K2tog tbl, k7, k2tog.

Row 10: Purl.

Row 11: K2tog tbl, k5, k2tog.

Row 12: Purl.

Row 13: K2tog tbl, k3, k2tog.

Row 14: Purl.
Row 15: K2tog tbl, k1, k2tog.
Row 16: Purl.
Row 17: Sl1, k2tog psso.
Make as many leaves as desired for centre of sunflower.

Making up
Press centre piece and stitch to centre of throw. Sew in two overlapping circles of leaves at edge of bobble insert. Add leaves. Make pompoms (see page 126) to stitch to outside edge of throw, plus one more for the centre.
Attach pompoms.

This box cushion is based on those that could be found in English inns. They are very easy to make as they have a top and a bottom to which side sections are added. Colour and design can be chosen to fit into a retro or modern décor.

Box cushion

THE ESSENTIALS

Measurements
40 x 40cm (16 x 16in) square

Materials
Rowan *Big Wool*, 100g/3½oz balls, approx 80m/87yd (wool)

   15 x White Hot (A)

Coloured yarn for weaving

10.00mm (US 15) needles

40 x 40cm (16 x 16in) square cushion pad with 5cm (2in) deep box sides

Large tapestry needle with big eye

Tension
10 sts and 18 rows to 10cm (4in) over Garter st using 10.00mm (US 15) needles.

Note
Measure the width, length, and depth of the cushion pad and alter the pattern to fit, if necessary.

Stitches used
Garter Stitch

Abbreviations
See page 136.

Special abbreviation
MB = Make Bobble as follows: knit into front then back of st twice, then front again. Turn, k5, turn, k5, turn, k5, turn, k5, turn, k5, turn, k5, slip 2nd, 3rd, 4th and 5th loops over first stitch.

Top and bottom (make two)
Cast on 36 sts using 10.00mm (US 15) needles and doubled yarn.
Row 1: Knit.
Row 2: Knit.
Continue in garter stitch for length required (approx 64 rows for size given)
Cast (bind) off.

Welt
With WS of bottom of cushion facing, pick up 36 sts of single yarn evenly along one side and work as follows:
Row 1 (RS): Knit.
Row 2: Purl.
Row 3: Knit.
Row 4: Purl.
Row 5: [K5, MB] 6 times.
Row 6: Purl.
Row 7: Knit.
Row 8: Purl.
Cast (bind) off.
Rep for other three sides.

Embellishments
With large needle and orange yarn, pick up garter stitches and overcast two straight lines across the cushion. Repeat with green yarn. Make 60cm (24in) of twisted cord using Big Wool. Divide into four equal lengths and use a large needle to anchor each into position at each corner of cushion. Knot ends and trim.

Making up
Match the top edge of each welt around the outer edge of the top cushion piece. With WS together and matching the bottom cushion piece, pin the top carefully to all four sides. Pin on the outside and not inside since heavy duty stitching is needed to accentuate the edge of the box shape, and the sharp edge will disappear if sewn up from inside. Using a large needle and yarn work backstitch from right to left to join.

BUTTON UP
Hand wash the cushion with the pad still enclosed to be sure that it will keep its shape. The box pad should be a fraction bigger than the cover enclosing it to obtain the proper 'buttoned' look.

For this rug, I-cord has been braided into a 'tabby' weave alternating with a 'false braid' of I-cord for accent and strength. Loop knitting has then been added, with a final outside edge of twice knit knitting.

Denim rug

THE ESSENTIALS

Measurements
60cm (24in) diameter

Materials
Rowan *Denim*, 50g/1¾oz balls, approx 25m/27yd (wool)

    10 x Nashville (A)

    10 x Ecru (B)

One pair size 3.00mm (US 2–3) double-pointed needles for I-cord

6.00mm (US 10) needles for loop and twice-knit knitting

Large safety pin

Some rubber bands

Needle for lacing

Tension
20 sts and 28 rows to 10 cm (4 in) over St st using 6.00mm (US 10) needles.

Note
The amount of I-cord required depends on the final size of the rug and how tightly the braid is made.

Stitches used
Stocking Stitch
Reverse Stocking Stitch

Abbreviations
See page 136.

Special Abbreviation
Loop = Loop Stitch as follows: insert needle into next st, wrap yarn round needle point and index finger of left hand 3 times clockwise, draw loops through the st. Slip these sts back onto the left hand needle and knit all loops as one st.

I-cord
Using double pointed needles, cast on 6 sts in A.
Row 1: Knit.
Row 2: Do not turn. Slide sts back to beg of needle and knit the row again. Continue until required length of cord is reached.
For the small rug 60cm (24in) in diameter, make 3 lengths of I-cord in A each 450cm (15ft) long and 2 lengths of I-cord in B each 450 cm (15ft) long

Loop Knitting
Using 6.00mm (US 10) needles and one strand of A and one of B together, cast on 11 sts.
Row 1: Knit
Row 2: *K1, loop; rep from * to last st, k1.
Row 3: Knit.
Row 4: K2, *loop, K1; rep from * to last stitch, k1.
Rep these 4 rows until required length is reached.
Cast (bind) off.

Twice Knit Knitting
(Cast on method, useful for when edges need to be fringed.)
Using 6.00mm (US 10) needles make a slip knot.
Row 1: Using the knit method, cast on the next st by knitting into the slip knot and placing the new st onto the left hand needle.

Next, insert the right hand needle into both of these two sts as though you were knitting two together, cast on placing the new st onto the left hand needle. (3 sts)
Continue casting on by inserting the right hand needle into the two last sts made, until 8 sts (or number of sts required) have been cast on.
Row 2: Knit.
Row 3: *K2tog, sl first st off needle keeping 2nd st on needle, K2tog using 2nd st not dropped and next following st on left hand needle; rep from * to last st. After final k2tog, knit into back of 2nd st before slipping off needle.
Rep row 3 until required length of edging has been reached.
To cast (bind) off, work as for a basic chain cast (bind) off. K3, lift first st over other two. Continue in this way to end, fasten off final 2 sts.

(Pattern continued on page 134)

COOL CURVE
The braided cords will lie flat if the braids are not sewn too tightly. The looped curves should be sewn on around the outside curve first, the inner curve drawn in so that it fits as flat as possible. Ease into and out of the curves. Lining the rug is also an option, if you wish.

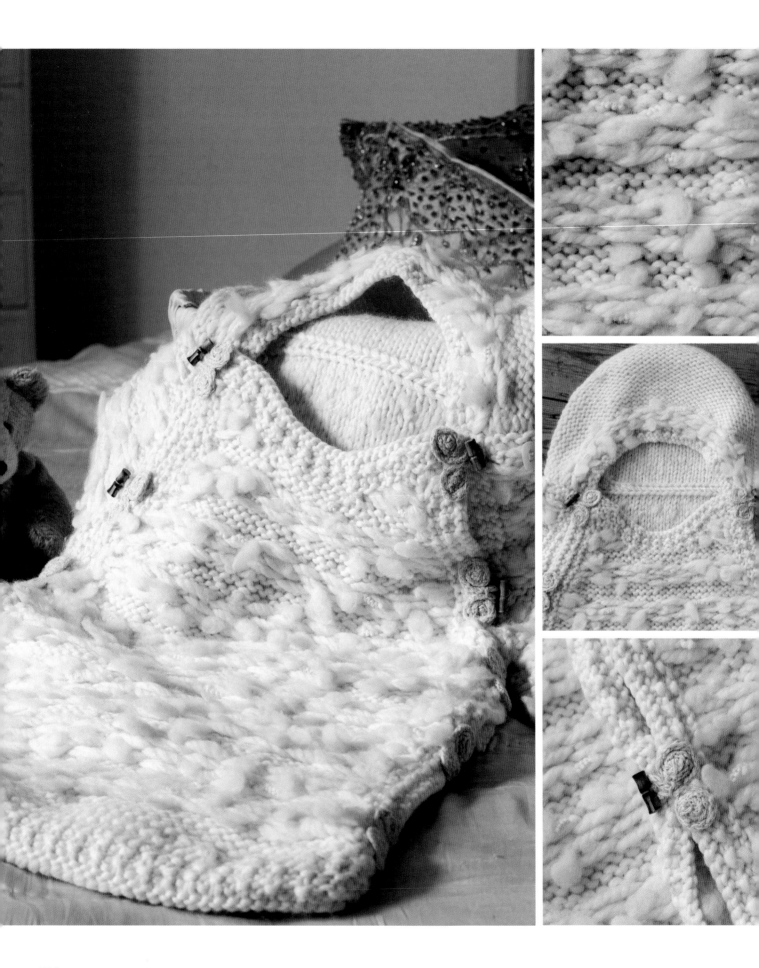

Baby pouch

This idea is inspired by the ways used by nomadic families to carry their babies. Since they were exposed to the elements, garments had to be warm and robust. Nowadays, many mothers are using these traditional pouches again.

THE ESSENTIALS

Measurements

For 1st size: width across back 40cm (16in); length 55cm (22in)

Materials

Rowan *Big Wool*, 100g/3½oz balls, approx 80m/87yd (wool)

    5 x White Hot 001 (A)

Rowan *Big Wool Tuft*, 50g/1¾oz balls, approx 25m/27yd (wool)

    5 x Frosty 055 (B)

8.00mm (US 11) needles

5.00mm (US 8) needles

Stitch holder

Scraps of cream 4-ply yarn for toggle fastening

12 buttons or toggles

Tension

12 sts and 14 rows to 10cm (4in) over pattern using 8.00mm (US 11) needles.

Note

For Medieval Knot, see page 128.

Stitches used

Stocking Stitch
Reverse Stocking Stitch
Fancy Stitch One (see right)
Fancy Stitch Two (see right)

Abbreviations

See page 136.

Fancy Stitch One

Worked in multiples of 6 sts.
Row 1 (RS): *Using A, p3, tie in B, p3; rep from * across the row leaving yarn in front of work.
Row 2 (WS): *Using A, k3, using B, k3; repeat from * across row leaving yarn at back of work.
Row 3: Rep row 1.
Row 4–6: Using A only cont. in Reverse St st for three rows.
These 6 rows form pattern.

Fancy Stitch Two

Worked in multiples of 2 sts.
Row 1 (WS): Knit.
Row 2: [K1, p1] to end of row.
Row 3: Knit.
Row 4: [K1, p1) to end of row.
Row 5: Knit.
These 5 rows form pattern.

Back

Using A and 8.00mm (US 11) needles, cast on 24 sts and work in garter st as follows:
Row 1 (RS): Knit.
Row 2: Knit.
Rows 3–10: Cast on 3 sts at beg of each row. (48 sts)
Tie in a marker thread at beginning and end of last row.
Work Fancy Stitch One patt six times, ending with WS row.
Cont with Fancy Stitch One patt while decreasing as follows:
Row 47: As Fancy Stitch One patt row 1.
Row 48: As Fancy Stitch One patt row 2.

Row 49: As Fancy Stitch One patt row 3.
Row 50 (WS): Knit.
Row 51: P2tog, purl to last 2 sts, p2tog. (46 sts)
Cont to work in Fancy Stitch One patt, dec 1 st in this way at each end of every following alt row until 20 sts remain, ending on a patt row 2.
Cast (bind) off.

Front

Using A and 8.00mm (US 11) needles, cast on 24 sts and work in garter st as follows:
Row 1 (RS): Knit.
Row 2: Knit.
Rows 3–10: Cast on 3 sts at beg of each row. (48 sts)
Tie in a marker thread at beginning and end of last row.
Cast off 3 sts at beg of next two rows, at the same time beginning to work Fancy Stitch One pattern. Complete Fancy Stitch One pattern 6 times in all. (36 rows)
Cont with Fancy Stitch One pattern while decreasing as follows:
Row 47: As Fancy Stitch One patt row 1.
Row 48: As Fancy Stitch One patt row 2.
Row 49: As Fancy Stitch One patt row 3.
Row 50 (WS): Knit.
Row 51: P2tog, purl to last 2 sts, p2tog. (46 sts)
Cont to work in Fancy Stitch One patt, dec 1 st in this way at each end of every following alt row until 24 sts remain, ending on a patt row 4.

Next row: K2tog, p6, purl next 8 sts, then place these sts onto a stitch holder, p6 sts, k2tog.
Next row: Working on first 7 sts only, sl 1, k1, psso, cont in patt to last 2 sts, k2tog. (5 sts)
Rep last row. (3 sts)
Next row: K3 tog.
Fasten off.
Leaving the centre 8 sts on holder, rep these last 2 rows for rem 7 sts.

Sleeves

Using A and 5.00mm (US 8) needles, cast on 21sts.
Row 1 (WS): Knit.
Row 2 (RS): Knit, inc. in 1st st and every following 4th st. (27 sts)
Row 3: Knit.
Row 4: Knit 2 inc. in next st., and every following 3rd st. (36 sts)
Row 5 (WS): Knit.
Row 16–17: Change to 8.00mm (US 11) needles and continue in Fancy Stitch One patt working pattern twice ending with a row 6 (WS).
Row 18 (RS): Continuing in Fancy Stitch One patt, sl1, k1, psso, pattern to last two sts, knit 2tog. (34 sts)
Row 19: Knit Fancy Stitch One patt.
Row 20: Sl1, k1, psso, patt to last two sts, k2tog. (32 sts)
Row 21 (WS): Knit.
Row 22 (RS): Sl1, k1, psso, patt to last two sts, k2tog. (30 sts)
Row 23: Knit.
Repeat 18–23 until 14 sts remain.

Shape neck

Next Row (RS): Cast (bind) off 5 sts. Patt to last two sts, k2tog.
Keeping this neck edge straight continue to dec one stitch at raglan edge on alt rows until 6 sts remain.
Cast (bind) off remaining 6 sts.
Reverse neck shapings for second sleeve.

Making up

Join back raglan seams to back raglan sleeve seams. Join sleeve seams from wrists to armpits.

Make side button band

With RS facing and using 5.00mm (US 8) needles and A, pick up and knit 82 sts up first side of back and along front raglan seam edge of sleeve.
Work Fancy Stitch Two patt once.
Cast (bind) off.
Rep button band for other side.

Make front button band

With RS facing and using 5.00mm (US 8) needles and A, pick up and knit 72 sts along front edge from marker thread to neck edge.
Work Fancy Stitch Two patt once.
Cast (bind) off.
Rep for remaining front edge.

Neck

With RS facing and using 5.00mm (US 8) needles and A, pick up and knit 4 sts from front band, 7 sts along neck edge, 8 sts on stitch holder, 7 sts along other neck edge and 4 sts from other front band.
Work Fancy Stitch Two patt once.
Cast (bind) off.

Joining back and front

With RS facing and using 5.00mm (US 8) needles and A, pick up and knit 60 sts on front, beginning from marker thread on one side, along increase rows, along cast on edge and continuing up to marker thread on opposite side.
Work Fancy Stitch Two patt once.
Cast (bind) off.
Rep for back.
With RS together backstitch two bottom edges together so that when the baby pouch is turned inside out the front now has a 'turtle' opening.
With front bands overlapping back bands, pin these two together placing pins to mark where buttons should be, spaced evenly from marking thread to neck opening, placing last 2 buttons 2.5cm (1in) apart at neck so neckline can be adjusted.
Add toggles and Medieval Knot loops or buttons and loops for fastening.

Hood (optional)

Using A and 5.00mm (US 8) needles, cast on 50 sts.
Row 1: Knit.
Row 2: Knit.
Row 3: K1, p1 to end.
Row 4: Knit.
Row 5: K1, p1 to end.
Row 6: Knit.
Change to 8.00mm (US 11) needles and work Fancy Stitch One patt once.
Next row (RS): Purl.
Next row: Knit.
Continue in reversed stocking stitch for a further 12 rows.
Bind off 2 sts at beg of next and every foll row until 18 sts remain.
Work straight until hood measures 31.5cm (12½in) from beg, ending with a WS row.
Cast (bind) off.
Press hood and stitch edges together before joining to neck.
Pin out entire garment very carefully and cover with a damp cloth. Leave to dry.

ALL SEASONS
Lightweight versions can be worked quite easily – choose your yarn and work a swatch before knitting up the final garment. Why not personalize your design by using your favourite colour?

This rug is made up of a combination of ribbons of plastic and all those orphaned balls of yarn. Although almost any yarn can be used, natural fibres seem to work best. This project is simple to make and environmentally friendly.

Recycled rug

THE ESSENTIALS

Measurements

150cm (60in) across

Materials

Rowan *Denim*, 50g/1¾oz balls, approx 93m/101yd (wool)

    7 x Nashville 225 (A)

    6 x 50g (1¾oz) balls of assorted colours. This is very dependant on the weight and tension of the knitted yarn as well as how the plastic is cut up into strips (B)

Plastic strips (C)

4.00–5.00mm (US 6–8) needles (select size to suit yarn)

Tapestry needle

Tension

Tension is not important on this project, but make a test swatch to select the right needles to get the look you want.

Stitches used

Garter Stitch

Notes

All yarn quantities are approximate as the choice of materials, as well as the needle size, will affect final amounts.

You will need 18 full diamonds and 12 half diamonds to complete each section. Six sections are needed to make up the hexagon.

The design can be based on any shape, but the diamond is versatile and makes up some wonderfully different patterns. The six-pointed star can be built up into a hexagon, which can be rearranged into the box or tumbling blocks pattern.

Abbreviations

See page 136.

Preparing the plastic

The plastic should all be the same weight. For the rug in the photograph, plastic grocery bags were cut up into strips 6–25mm (¼–1in) wide and simply knotted together. Knotting the lengths gives a textured effect, and they can be trimmed with scissors after the rug is completed. The narrower the width of the strips, the more pronounced the pattern. For a more 'woven look' opt for a wider measurement. Wind the knotted lengths into balls just like ordinary yarn. If the plastic used is particularly shiny, anchor the balls together with elastic bands until you are ready to use them. This octagonal rug is made up of six triangular pieces sewn together at the end to make up the whole.

Preparing the yarn

Short lengths of yarn can be made up into one continuous length by knotting them together. This will produce an exciting random design, with the knots becoming a feature. The yarns should be of similar weight – the rug in the photograph uses Rowan Handknit Cotton, 100% cotton in DK weight, for colour with Rowan Denim for contrast. Interest is generated by the use of colours and the manner in which the geometric shapes are placed.

Diamond

With a suitable size of needle and B, cast on 3 sts.

Row 1: Pick up C together with B, k3.

Row 2: Inc by knitting into both front and back of first and last stitch. (5 sts)

Cont to increase in this manner on every row until 35 sts are on the needle. Break off B and join in A, working A with C begin to dec as follows:

Next row: Sl 1, k1, psso, knit to last 2 sts, k2tog. (33 sts)

Continue to decrease in this manner on every row until 3 sts rem on needle.

Next row: Sl 1, k2tog, psso.

Fasten off.

Half diamond

With a suitable size of needle and A, cast on 3 sts.

Row 1: Pick up C together with A, k3.

Row 2: Inc by knitting into both front and back of first and last stitch. (5 sts)

Cont to inc in this manner on every row until 35 sts are on the needle.

Cast (bind) off.

Making up

Weave in ends. Sew each section together in the desired shape using both plastic and yarn together – although it is possible to use the yarn on its own, it will not blend in as well.

CLEAN MACHINE

Regular vacuuming or stiff brushing of both sides will remove most surface dirt before it becomes embedded. The rug should also be turned every so often. Spots and stains should be removed immediately with an absorbent cloth, and mild shampoos can also be used.

Embell

ishments

On the following pages you will find lots of ideas to inspire you to add further embellishments and decoration to your finished projects. Experiment with each one to add your own unique touch to any knitted piece. Many of these are inspired by different eras – find one to suit you.

BINDING WITH PIPING CORD

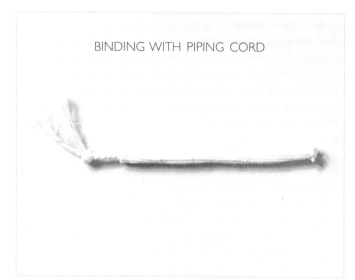

GIMP EDGING

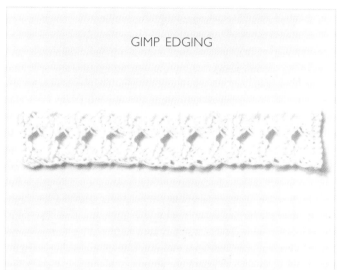

BRAIDED CORD

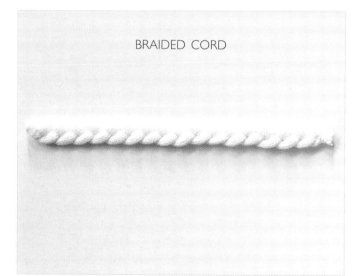

CASTLE EDGE KEEPING

BINDING WITH PIPING CORD

· Work a strip of stocking stitch binding as described on page 33, wide enough to enclose manufactured piping cord.
· Fold binding in half lengthways and insert piping cord tight against fold line.
· Slipstitch free edges to project.

PIPE DREAMS

Piping is ideal to use when you want to add a professional look to the edges of a cushion cover or counterpane.

BRAIDED CORD

In general between 30–60cm (1–2ft) lengthwise is lost for every 122cm (4ft) that is braided. Allow an extra 18–20cm (7–8in) more for each round if the spiral is continuous. A further allowance of 18–20 cm (7–8in) should be allowed for the ends.

For floor rugs, braids should be oversewn to avoid the centre rising up to a point.

GIMP EDGING

Cast on multiples of 6. Knit one row.
Row 1: *k1, yo three times, rep from * to end.
Row 2: [sl1, drop yos], repeat five times more until there are 6 sts on right hand needle. Pass these 6 sts back to left hand needle. Pass the last three sts to the front of first three sts. Do not twist. Next, knit these stitches off in order. Repeat to end of row.
Row 3: Knit.
Row 4: Knit.
Row 5 and 6: Repeat rows one and two.
Row 7 and 8: Knit.

CASTLE KEEP EDGING

Cast on 6 sts.
Rows 1–3: Knit.
Row 4: Cast on 3 sts, k to end. (9 sts)
Rows 5–7: Knit.
Row 8: Cast on 3 sts, k to end. (12 sts)
Rows 9–15: Knit.
Row 16: Bind off 3 sts, purl to end. (9 sts)
Row 17: Knit.
Row 18: Purl.
Row 19: Knit.
Row 20: Bind (cast) off 3 sts, purl to end. (6 sts)
These 20 rows form pattern.
Rep these 20 rows for desired length of edging.

TWICE KNIT A

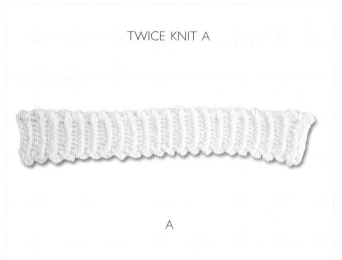

A

TWICE KNIT B

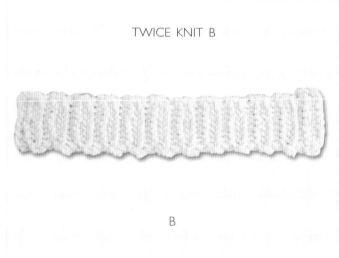

B

RAILROAD AND SIDING EDGE: QUAKER VARIATION

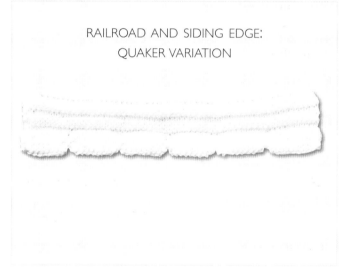

TWICE KNIT VERSION A

To cast on
Make a slip knot.
Row 1: Using knit method, cast on 1 st by knitting into slip knot and placing the new st onto left hand needle.
Next, insert right hand needle into both of these 2 sts as though k2tog, cast on 1 st, place new st onto left hand needle. (3 sts)
Continue casting on by inserting right hand needle into last 2 sts made, until 8 sts (or any number of sts required) have been cast on.
Row 2: Knit.

To knit
Row 1: *K2tog, slip first st off needle keeping 2nd st on needle, k2tog again using the 2nd st not dropped and the next following st on left hand needle; rep from * to last st, k into back of 2nd st before slipping off needle.
Row 2: As row 1.

To cast (bind) off
Work as for a basic chain bind off.
*K3, lift first st over the other two; rep to end, fasten off final 2 sts.

TWICE KNIT VERSION B

To cast on
Make a slip knot.
Row 1: Using knit method, cast on 1 st by knitting into slip knot and placing the new st onto left hand needle.
Next, insert right hand needle into both of these 2 sts as though k2tog, cast on 1 st, place new st onto left hand needle. (3 sts)
Continue casting on by inserting right hand needle into last 2 sts made, until 8 sts (or any number of sts required) have been cast on.
Row 2: Knit.

To knit
Row 1: *K2tog, slip first st off needle keeping 2nd st on needle, k2tog again using the 2nd st not dropped and the next following st on left hand needle; rep from * to last st, k into back of 2nd st before slipping off needle.
Row 2: As row 1.
Row 3: Knit.
Row 4: Knit.

These four rows form the pattern for version two of twice knit knitting.
Repeat these four rows until the desired length is reached.

To cast (bind) off
Work as for a basic chain bind off.
*K3, lift first st over the other two; rep to end, fasten off final 2 sts.

RAILROAD AND SIDING EDGE: QUAKER VARIATION

To cast on
Row 1 (RS): Knit.
Row 2 (WS): Purl.
Row 3: Knit.
Row 4: Purl.
Row 5 (RS): Purl.
Row 6: Knit.
Row 7: Purl.
Row 8 (WS): Purl.
Row 9: Knit.
Row 10: Purl.
Row 11 (RS): Purl.
Row 12: Knit.
Row 13: Purl.
Work in reverse stocking stitch for **twice** the desired width of border.
Cast (bind) off.

Fold border in half, purl side out. Break yarn leaving a long tail for next stage.
Thread the end into a yarn needle and with WS facing pick up one st from bound off edge and one corresponding st from purled edge. At every 10th st, pass yarn over top of border and pull tight to shape curve.

PLEAT A

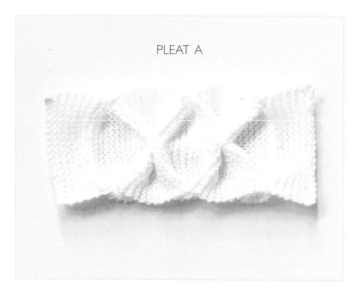

PLEAT B

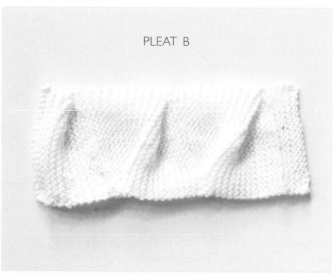

PLEAT C

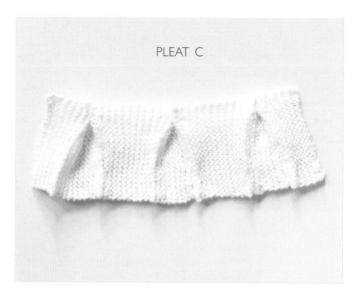

ROLLING SCROLL INSERTION AND EDGE

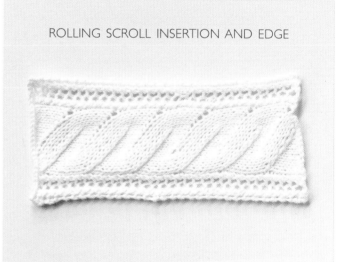

PLEAT

Knit a strip of garter stitch to desired height. For pleat A, pinch 2.5cm (1in) at the top and bottom of knitted fabric at 5cm (2in) intervals. Stitch in place at the halfway point between each pleat, pinch 2.5cm (1in) in the centre at 5cm (2in) intervals. Stitch in place. Continue for length of edging.

For pleat B, work as for pleat C. Then, at the bottom edge, repeat the step by pinching 2.5cm (1in) of fabric at the halfway point between the two top edge pleats. Stitch in place. Continue for length of edging.

For pleat C, pinch 2.5cm (1in) of fabric at 5cm (2in) intervals at one edge of fabric, stitch in place.

ROLLING SCROLL INSERTION AND EDGE

Pattern is in multiples of 20+6 sts.
Row 1: P1, k2, yo, sl1, k1, psso, p1, yo, k3, sl1, k1, psso, k9, p1, k2, yo, sl, k1, psso, p1.
Row 2: K1, p2, yo, p2tog, k1, p8, p1dec. (next st is a simple dec p1, with yarn in front [wyif] slip next stitch knit-wise, then slip both stitches back to left hand needle, pass sl st over purl st. Transfer back to right hand needle), p3, yo, p1, k1, p2, yo, p2tog, k1.
Row 3: P1, k2, yo, sl1, k1, psso, p1, k2, yo, k3, sl1, k1, psso, k7, p1, k2, yo, sl1k1, psso, p1.
Row 4: K1, p2, yo, p2tog, k1, p6, p1dec, p3, yo, p3, k1, p2, yo, p2tog, k1.
Row 5: P1, k2, yo, sl1k1, psso, p1, k4, yo, k3, sl1, k1, psso, k5, p1, k2, yo, sl1, k1, psso, p1.
Row 6: K1, p2, yo, p2tog, k1, p4, p1dec, p3, yo, p5, k1, p2, yo, p2tog, k1.
Row 7: P1, k2, yo, sl1, k1, psso, p1, k6, yo, k3, sl1k1, psso, k3, p1, k2, yo, sl1, k1, psso, p1.
Row 8: K1, p2, yo, p2tog, k1, p2, p1dec, p3, yo, p7, k1, p2, yo, p2tog, k1.
Row 9: P1, k2, yo, sl1, k1, psso, p1, k8, yo, k3, sl1k1, psso, k1, p1, k2, yo, sl1, k1, psso, p1.
Row 10: K1, p2, yo, p2tog, p1dec, p3, yo, p9, k1, p2, yo, p2tog, k1.
These 10 rows form the pattern, repeat until desired length is reached.

PLEATED KILT

BOXED PLEAT

PLEATED KILT

Pattern is in multiples of 20 sts.
Row 1: K1, p9, k9, p1.
Row 2: K2, p8, k8, p2.
Row 3: K3, p7, k7, p3.
Row 4: K4, p6, k6, p4.
Row 5: K5, p5, k5, p5.
Row 6: K6, p4, k4, p6.
Row 7: K7, p3, k3, p7.
Row 8: K8, p2, k2, p8.
Row 9: K9, p1, k1, p9.
Row 10: P9, k1, p1, k9.
Row 11: P8, k2, p2, k8.
Row 12: P7, k3, p3, k7.
Row 13: P6, k4, p4, k6.
Row 14: P5, k5, p5, k5.
Row 15: P4, k6, p6, k4.
Row 16: P3, k7, p7, k3.
Row 17: P2, k8, p8, k2.
Row 18: P1, k9, p9, k1.
Row 19–38: Repeat rows 1–18.
These rows form pattern.
To create pleat, pinch at regular intervals in the same direction – width to be of knitter's choice. Sew into place. Stocking stitch binding can be added at top edge.

BOXED PLEAT

Pattern is in multiples of 20 sts.
Row 1: K1, p9, k9, p1.
Row 2: K2, p8, k8, p2.
Row 3: K3, p7, k7, p3.
Row 4: K4, p6, k6, p4.
Row 5: K5, p5, k5, p5.
Row 6: K6, p4, k4, p6.
Row 7: K7, p3, k3, p7.
Row 8: K8, p2, k2, p8.
Row 9: K9, p1, k1, p9.
Row 10: P9, k1, p1, k9.
Row 11: P8, k2, p2, k8.
Row 12: P7, k3, p3, k7.
Row 13: P6, k4, p4, k6.
Row 14: P5, k5, p5, k5.
Row 15: P4, k6, p6, k4.
Row 16: P3, k7, p7, k3.
Row 17: P2, k8, p8, k2.
Row 18: P1, k9, p9, k1.
Row 19–38: Repeat rows 1–18.
To create box pleat, pinch at regular intervals, and bring two pinched points to meet at a centre point. Stitch in place. Stocking stitch binding can be added at top edge.

REVERSE STOCKING STITCH:
PLEATED AND SMOCKED

APPLE LEAF LACE

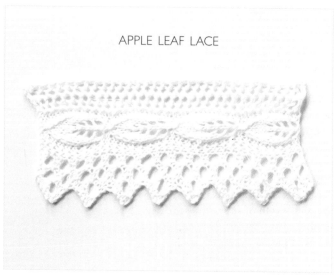

VINTAGE LACE EDGING

REVERSE STOCKING STITCH: PLEATED AND SMOCKED

Cast on stitches in a number that is a multiple of 6 sts.
Continue in 1/5 rib knit (purl 5 sts, knit 1 st, then repeat and finish with 5 purled stitches).
Next row: Continue in 1/5 rib (knit 5 sts, purl one st, then repeat and finish with 5 knit sts).
Repeat last two rows for length required. Put on hold.
Pull the ribs together and stitch the two rib rows as shown in the embellishments.
Move up every six rows and sew ribs to form diamonds.
Size and length of smocking with be determined by the number of stitches in multiples of 6 and length of final smocked piece.

VINTAGE LACE EDGING

Special abbreviation
Dot = Make dot as follows: pass next 2 sts onto spare needle, wind yarn around these two sts on spare needle 3 times, knit both sts.

Cast on 7 sts.
Row 1: Sl1, k2, yo, k2tog, k2.
Row 2: Sl1, k1, yo, k2, yo, k2tog, k1.
Row 3: Sl1, k2, [yo, k1, yo, k1] into next stitch, k1, p1, k2.
Row 4: Sl1, k7, yo, k2tog, k1.
Row 5: Sl1, k2, yo, k2tog, [Dot] twice, k2.
Row 6: Cast (bind) off 4 sts, k3, yo, k2tog, k1. (7 sts)
These 6 rows form pattern.
Rep these 6 rows for desired length of edging.

APPLE LEAF LACE

Cast on 19 sts.
Knit one row then proceed as follows:
Row 1: Sl1, k1, [yo, k2tog] twice, p2, [k1, yo] twice, k1, p2, k2, yo twice, k2tog, yo twice, k2. (24 sts)
Row 2: K3, p1, k2, p1, k4, p5, k2, p5, k1.
Row 3: Sl1, k1, [yo, k2tog] twice, p2, k2, yo, k1, yo, k2, p2, k9. (26 sts)
Row 4: K11, p7, k2, p5, k1.
Row 5: Sl1, k1, [yo, k2tog] twice, p2, k3, yo, k1, yo, k3, p2, k2, [yo twice, k2tog], 3 times, k1. (31 sts)
Row 6: K3, p1, [k2, p1] twice, k4, p9, k2, p5, k1.
Row 7: Sl1, k1, [yo, k2tog] twice, p2, k4, yo, k1, yo, k4, p2, k12. (32 sts)
Row 8: Cast (bind) off 5 sts, k8, p11, k2, p5, k1. (27 sts)
Row 9: Sl1 , k1, [yo, k2tog] twice, p2, sl1, k1, psso, k7, k2tog, p2, k2, [yo twice, k2tog] twice, k1. (28 sts)
Row 10: K3, p1, k2, p1, k4, p9, k2, p5, k1.
Row 11: Sl1, k1, [yo, k2tog] twice, p2, sl 1, k1, psso, k5, k2tog, p2, k9. (26 sts)
Row 12: K11, p7, k2, p5, k1.
Row 13: Sl1, k1, [yo, k2tog] twice, p2, sl1, k1, psso, k3, k2tog, p2, k2, [yo twice, k2tog] 3 times, k1. (27 sts)
Row 14: K3, p1, [k2, p1] twice, k4, p5, k2, p5, k1.
Row 15: Sl1, k1, [yo, k2tog] twice, p2, sl 1, k1, psso, k1, k2tog, p2, k12. (25 sts)
Row 16: K14, p3, k2, p5, k1.
Row 17: Sl1, k1, [yo, k2tog] twice, p2, k3tog, p2, k12. (23 sts)
Row 18: Bind off 4 sts, k12, p5, k1. (19 sts)
These 18 rows form pattern.
Rep these 18 rows for desired length of edging.

GODMOTHER'S EDGING

SHARK'S TOOTH EDGING

MEDIUM POINTED EDGING

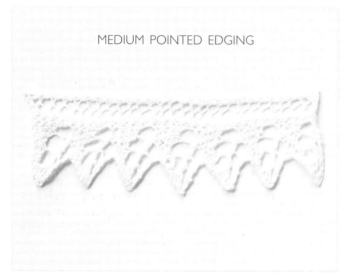

LACE RUFFLE

GODMOTHER'S EDGING

Cast on 20 sts.
Knit 1 row then proceed as follows:
Row 1: K2, [yo, k2tog] 8 times, yo, k2. (21 sts)
Row 2: Knit.
Row 3: K5, [yo, k2tog,] 7 times, yo, k2. (22 sts)
Row 4: Knit.
Row 5: K8, [yo, k2tog] 6 times, yo, k2. (23 sts)
Row 6: Knit.
Row 7: K11, [yo, k2tog] 5 times, yo, k2. (24 sts)
Row 8: Knit.
Row 9: K14, [yo, k2tog], 4 times, yo, k2. (25 sts)
Row 10: Knit.
Row 11: K17, [yo, k2tog] 3 times, yo, k2. (26 sts)
Row 12: Knit.
Row 13: K20, [yo, k2tog] twice, yo, k2. (27 sts)
Row 14: Knit.
Row 15: K23, yo, k2tog, yo, k2. (28 sts)
Rows 16–17: Knit.
Row 18: Bind off 8 sts, knit to end. (20 sts)
These 18 rows form pattern.
Rep these 18 rows for desired length of edging.

MEDIUM POINTED EDGING

Cast on 10 sts.
Knit one row then proceed as follows:
Row 1: Sl1, k2, yo, k2tog, k1, [yo twice, k2tog] twice.
Row 2: Sl1, k1, p1, k2, p1, k3, yo, k2tog, k1.
Row 3: Sl1, k2, yo, k2tog, k3, [yo, twice, k2tog] twice.
Row 4: Sl1, k1, p1, k2, p1, k5, yo, k2tog, k1.
Row 5: Sl1, k2, yo, k2tog, k5, [yo, twice, k2tog] twice.
Row 6: Sl1. k1, p1, k2, p1, k7, yo, k2tog, k1.
Row 7: Sl1, k2, yo, k2tog, k11.
Row 8: Bind off 6 sts, k6, (7 sts on right hand needle) yo, k2tog, k1. (10 sts)
These 8 rows form pattern.
Rep these 8 rows for desired length of edging.

SHARK'S TOOTH EDGING

This is a very easy edging pattern for beginners.
Cast on 8 sts.
Knit one row then proceed as follows:
Row 1: S11, k1, [yo, k2tog] twice, yo, k2. (9 sts)
Row 2: K2, yo, k2, [yo, k2tog] twice, k1. (10 sts)
Row 3: Sl1, k1, [yo, k2tog] twice, k2, yo, k2. (11 sts)
Row 4: K2, yo, k4, [yo, k2tog] twice, k1. (12 sts)
Row 5: Sl1, k1, [yo, k2tog] twice, k4, yo, k2. (13 sts)
Row 6: K2, yo, k6, [yo, k2tog] twice, k1. (14 sts)
Row 7: Sl1, k1, [yo, k2tog] twice, k6, yo, k2. (15 sts)
Row 8: K2, yo, k8, [yo, k2tog] twice, k8, yo, k2. (16 sts)
Row 9: Sl1, k1, [yo, k2tog] twice, k8, yo, k2. (17 sts)
Row 10: K2, yo, k10, [yo, k2tog] twice, k1. (18 sts)
Row 11: Sl1, k1, [yo, k2tog] twice, k10, yo, k2. (19 sts)
Row 12: Bind off 11 sts, k2, [yo, k2tog] twice, k1. (8 sts)
These 12 rows make up the pattern.
Rep these 12 rows for desired length of edging.

LACE RUFFLE

Pattern is in multiples of 3+1 sts.
Row 1. K1-b, (knit onto back of stitch, * p2, k1-b, rep from *.
Row 2. P1, * k1-b, k1,p1, rep from *
Continue until desired length is reached.
Next row, k1-b * drop next stitch from needle, p1, k1-b rep from *.
Cast (bind) off. Unravel the dropped stitches to beginning of cast on row. This edge can either be worked separately cast (bound) off and then sewn to another edge. Or, carried on to continue with knitting for another garment. Either leave frill as it is without starching, or pin out and starch.

FUR FRINGE

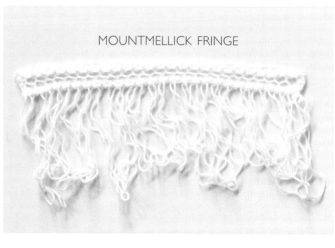

MOUNTMELLICK FRINGE

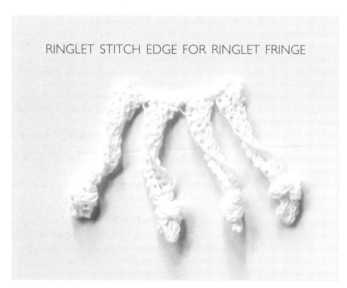

RINGLET STITCH EDGE FOR RINGLET FRINGE

FRINGE

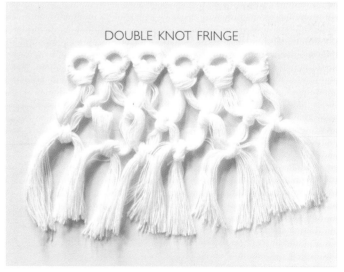

DOUBLE KNOT FRINGE

FUR FRINGE

Sometimes known as loop knitting, this is a decorative method of finishing used for many items of knitting. It consists of a series of loops, made by wrapping the yarn around one or two fingers. These are then knitted into the row as the row itself is knitted.

Special abbreviation
Loop 1 = Make loop as follows: insert needle into next st without knitting it. Place two fingers under the point of right hand needle, wrap yarn around fingers and needle 3 times clockwise. Now, as if to knit, draw loops through stitch on left hand needle, place back on left hand needle and knit all loops together as one.

Cast on an odd number of sts.
Row 1: Knit.
Row 2: *K1, Loop 1; rep from * to last st, k1.
Row 3: Knit.
Row 4: K2 * Loop 1, k1; rep from * to last st, k1.
These 4 rows form pattern.
Rep these 4 rows for desired length of edging.

RINGLET STITCH EDGE FOR RINGLET FRINGE

Special abbreviation
MR = Make ringlet as follows: p2, slip both sts back onto left hand needle, keeping yarn in front, pass yarn to back of work, slip sts back to right hand needle.

Cast on 14 sts.
Row 1 and every alt row: Purl.
Row 2: Knit.
Row 3: K6, * MR; rep from * to last st, k1.
These 2 rows form the pattern
Rep these 2 rows for desired length of edging.

MOUNTMELLICK FRINGE

Cast on 12 sts.
Row 1: *[yo, k2tog, k1] 4 times.
Row 2: As row 1.
These 2 rows form pattern.
Rep these 2 rows for desired length of edging.
Next row: Bind off 5 sts, break off yarn and draw end through last st on right hand needle. Slip the remaining 6 sts off left hand needle and unravel them entire length of fringe.

FRINGE

Cut a piece of cardboard about 20cm (8in) wide and half as long as specified instructions for finished strands. Wind yarn loosely around cardboard, cut across one end when card is filled. Repeat several times and then start fringing; you can wind more strands as you need them. Hold the number of strands specified for 1 knot of fringe together and fold in half. With crochet hook, draw folded end through space or stitch. Pull loose ends through folded section and draw knit up tightly.

DOUBLE KNOT FRINGE

Cut a piece of cardboard about 20cm (8in) wide and half as long as specified instructions for finished strands. Wind yarn loosely around cardboard, cut across one end when card is filled. Repeat several times and then start fringing; you can wind more strands as you need them. Hold the number of strands specified for 1 knot of fringe together and fold in half. With crochet hook, draw folded end through space or stitch. Pull loose ends through folded section and draw knit up tightly. Alternate and knot a second row as shown and repeat as desired.

POMPOM

MARIGOLD

TASSEL

SUNFLOWER

STEM

POMPOM

Cut two cardboard circles each 5.5cm (2¼in) in diameter. Cut a centre hole 2.5cm (1in) in diameter in each circle. Thread yarn needle with 4 lengths of yarn, each 180cm (72in) long. Holding circles together, pass needle through centre hole, around outside edge and through centre hole again until circle is thickly and evenly covered all around. Do not pull yarn too tight. Using very sharp scissors, cut yarn between the edges of the two circles.

Take a 60cm (24in) length of yarn, and fold in half to a 30cm (12in) double-strand length. Slip yarn between cardboard circles, pull up tightly and tie firmly. Remove cardboard circles and fluff out pompom. Trim yarn ends with scissors to even the sphere shape.

MARIGOLD

Cast on 9 sts (or multiple of 3 sts). Knit these 9 sts.
Row 1 (WS): Knit sts 1–3 as for Fur Fringe (see page 125), knit to last three sts. Turn. Having yarn at back of work, sl1 st off right hand needle onto left hand needle. Bring yarn to front of work and slip the sl st back onto right hand needle. WHEN TURNING ALWAYS SLIP FIRST ST IN THIS MANNER TO PREVENT A HOLE.
Row 2: Knit to end of row.
Row 3: Knit sts 1–3 as for Fur Fringe. Turn.
Row 4: Knit.
Row 5: Knit sts 1–3 as for Fur Fringe. Knit to end of row.
Row 6: Knit.
These six rows form the pattern. Repeat eleven times more to complete the circle.
Next row: Cast (bind) off. Leave yarn for sewing up. Run a line of sts around centre hole and pull tight to close hole. Complete flower by sewing up two edges.
With tapestry needle embellish and cover this knitted centre with French knots to emphasize flower seeds.

STEM

To make, follow instructions on page 33, omitting instruction to insert piping cord. Fold straight binding over and neatly stitch along edge either by hand or by machine. The stem is a hollow version of the stiffer I-cord.

TASSEL

Cut two cardboard pieces the length of tassel desired. Holding cardboard together, place a 30cm (12in) length of yarn across top of cardboard. Wind yarn several times around cardboard.
Tie strands tightly together around top. Using sharp scissors, cut yarn between two cardboard pieces. Wrap a piece of yarn tightly around strands a few times about 2.5cm (1in) below top, securing ends with a knot. Trim ends of tassel.

SUNFLOWER

Special abbreviation
MB = Make a bobble as follows: knit into front and back and front of next stitch. Turn and purl three turn and k.3, turn and p1, ptog, turn and k2tog. Repeat.
Loop = see page 125.

Cast on 3 sts. Knit.
Row 1 (RS): Inc in 1st st, k1, inc in last st. (5sts)
Row 2 (WS): Loop 1, k1, Loop 1, k1, Loop 1.
Row 3 (RS): Inc in first st, k3, inc in last st. (7sts)
Row 4 (WS): Loop 1, k1, Loop 1, k1, Loop 1, k1, Loop 1.
Row 5 (RS): Inc in first st, k5, inc in last st. (9sts)
Row 6 (WS): Loop 1, k1, Loop 1, k1, Loop 1, k1, Loop 1, k1, Loop 1.
Row 7 (RS): Inc in first st, k1, MB, k1, MB, k1, MB, k1, inc in last st. (11sts)
Row 8 (WS): Loop first 3 sts, k5, Loop last 3 sts.
Row 9 (RS): Inc in first st, k1, MB, k1, MB, k1, MB, k1, MB, k1, inc in last st. (13 sts)
Row 10 (WS): Loop first 3 sts, MB, k1, MB, k1, MB, k1, MB, Loop last three sts.
Row 11 (RS): K2tog, k1, MB, k1, MB, k1, MB, k1, MB, k1, k2tog. (11sts)
Row 12 (WS): Loop first 3 sts, k5, Loop last three sts.
Row 13 (RS): K2tog, k1, MB, k1, MB, k1, MB, k1, k2tog (9 sts)
Row 14 (WS): Loop first 3 sts, k3, Loop last three sts.
Row 15 (RS): K2tog, k1, MB, k1, MB, k1, k2tog. (7sts)
Row 16 (WS): Loop first 3 sts, k1, Loop last three sts.
Row 17 (RS): K2tog, k3, k2tog (5 sts)
Row 18 (WS): Work all 5 sts in Loop st.
Row 19 (RS): K2tog, k1, k2tog. (3 sts)
Row 20: K3 sts.
Row 21: Cast (bind) off.

DAISY

RINGWORK TECHNIQUE I

MEDIEVAL KNOT

TOGGLE FASTENING

RINGWORK TECHNIQUE II

RINGWORK TECHNIQUE III

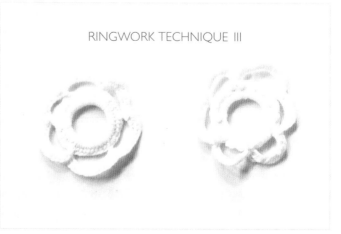

DAISY

Cut Rowan tape into three equal lengths of approx 90cm (36in) and braid.

If a thicker or longer braid is required double or triple the cut lengths and cut lengths longer. Braid all cut lengths – either braid each section separately and then braid these, or braid all 6/9 lengths together. Braid evenly.

Using approx 30cm (12in) of braided tape (or more if wished) coil this into a circle to represent a flower circle and stitch securely at the back.

Use remainder of braided tape for petals. Loop them evenly around and behind the centre flower and stitch each loop into place. The Vintage floor rug has 9 braided lengths of yarn. The Daisy illustrated opposite uses only 3 lengths. With spare Rowan *4-ply* or *Glace* dot centre of flower with large French Knots (more than three twists around the needle).

MEDIEVAL KNOT

With brown twine or yarn, crochet or knit a fairly tight chain approx 30cm (12in) long. If the tension is too loose or sizing is changed, adjust accordingly to create the closures. Follow diagram shown opposite for design.

RINGWORK TECHNIQUES

First make a ring by wrapping yarn chosen in the project fifteen times round the first two fingers of either hand (the number of times can be between 10 and 20, depending on the thickness of yarn and/or thickness of ring required).

Cut yarn leaving a good length (approx ⅓yd/m) to be threaded onto a tapestry needle.

Removing all fifteen rings carefully from fingers and working from left to right, begin to buttonhole (blanket stitch) all fifteen rings until the circle has been completely covered, making sure buttonholing lies on outer edge of ring and not inner edge of ring.

To create a stiffer ring, repeat this once more by inserting point of needle into previous buttonholes making sure these lie on outer edge.

Next, with needle and yarn working once more on outer edge of ring, work six outside loops equidistant to each other, anchoring each loop into the base of the outside ring of buttonholes.

Buttonhole all six loops twice over. These will represent the petals of your flower.

If a second layer is required, wrap the yarn around the thumb and repeat everything above. This will give you a centre to your flower.

	Twined Cushion Cover	Quilted Baby Blanket	Whitework Cushion	Vintage Floor Rug	Lace Leaf Throw	Lace & Eyelet Bolster	Lace & Flower Décor	Honeycomb Throw	Candlewick Cushion
Apple Leaf Lace		●	●		●		●		●
Binding with Piping Cord		●	●	●		●			●
Castle Keep Edging		●	●	●	●			●	●
Daisy		●	●	●		●			●
Fringe & Double Knot Fringe		●	●	●		●			●
Fur Fringe		●	●	●		●		●	●
Gimp Edging		●				●			
Godmother's Edging		●	●		●		●	●	●
Marigold		●	●	●		●		●	
Medieval Knot	●		●			●			●
Medium Point Edging		●	●		●		●	●	●
Mountmellick Fringe			●		●	●	●		●
Braided Cord		●		●		●			
Pleat		●	●			●		●	●
Pleated Kilt Pattern		●	●						
Pompom	●					●		●	
Railroad and Siding Edge (Quaker Variation)		●	●	●	●				●
Reverse Stocking Stitch		●	●						
Ringlet Fringe			●	●	●	●		●	
Ringwork Technique			●	●	●		●	●	
Rolling Scroll Insertion and Edge		●	●					●	●
Shark Tooth Edging		●	●	●	●		●	●	●
Sunflower		●	●	●		●		●	
Tassel	●	●		●		●			
Twice Knit				●		●			
Lace Ruffle		●	●		●		●	●	●
Vintage Lace Edging		●	●		●		●	●	●

Basketweave Cushion	Rag Rug Sampler	Classic Baby Blanket	Art Deco Quilt	The Garden Plot Counterpane	Ruffled Cushion	Circular Throw	Box Cushion	Denim Rug	Baby Pouch	Recycled Rug
		●		●						
					●		●			
		●	●	●			●			
	●	●	●	●		●	●	●		
	●	●	●					●		
	●	●	●					●		
		●		●						
					●				●	
●									●	
		●		●			●			
	●	●	●		●		●			
		●	●	●	●		●	●		
					●		●			
		●	●	●		●	●			
		●	●	●			●			
		●		●						
	●			●		●	●			
	●	●		●						
		●		●						
		●		●			●			
									●	
●	●				●		●			
	●	●			●			●		
		●		●			●			
		●		●			●			

Quilted baby blanket
(Continued from page 33)

Making up

Attach piping cord to RS of main body of knitted fabric matching edges with cord facing inwards. Pin in place and machine or hand stitch in place on top of existing line of stitches to all four sides of main body of fabric. Trim away excess wadding and press lightly. Turn under so that piping is now the new edge of the cover.

Apply a quilt edging from the gallery or embellishments now if desired. Attach the edging carefully by sewing closely to the underside of the new edge of the piping cord. The photograph shows 10 sts garter stitch edging and store-bought lace.

A lining fabric can now be added to cover the reverse of the work completely. Choose a pre-shrunk fabric and cut to same size as the baby blanket plus 3cm (1⅛in) all round for a seam. Press this seam allowance under and slip stitch into place.

WARMING TRENDS

Another and lighter alternative to wadding would be to line the knitted cover with a piece of lawn fabric, for example. Pin and then baste before quilting. The idea of quilting knitted fabric can be extended to other nursery items such as cushion covers and playpen mats.

Lacy leaf throw
(Continued from page 44)

Row 4: Knit to last 6 sts, p2, k1, p1, k2.
Row 5: Sl1, p1, k2tog, yo twice, k2tog tbl, k8, [yo, k2tog] 6 times, yo, k2.
Row 6: Knit to last 6 sts, p1, [k1, p1] into previous yo twice, p1, k2.
Row 7: Sl1, p1, k 15, [yo, k2tog] 5 times, yo, k2.
Row 8: Knit to last 6 sts, p2, k1, p1, k2.
Row 9: Sl1, p1, k2tog, yo twice, k2tog, tbl, k14, [yo, k2tog] 4 times, yo, k2.
Row 10: Knit to last 6 sts, p1, [k1, p1] into previous yo twice, p1, k2.
Row 11: Sl1, p1, k21, [yo, k2tog] 3 times, yo, k2.
Row 12: Knit to last 6 sts, p2, k1, p1, k2.
Row 13: Sl1, p1, k2tog, yo twice, k2tog, tbl, k20, [yo, k2tog] twice, yo, k2.
Row 14: K to last 6 sts, p1, [k1, p1] into yo, p1, k2.
Row 15: Sl1, p1, k27, yo, k2tog, yo, k2.
Row 16: Knit to last 6 sts, p2, k1, p1, k2.
Row 17: Sl1, p1, k2tog, yo twice, k2tog, tbl, knit to end of row
Row 18: Bind off 8 sts, knit to last 6 sts, p1, [k1,p1] into yo, p1, k2.
These 18 rows form the pattern.
When repeating these last 18 rows remember to knit the 4 row pattern of the open work insertion panel after each repetition.

Making up

Block and press each panel separately. Block and press each border so that the holes open out. Pin into position and sew by hand using stab stitches, which blend better into a knitted background.

Lace and flower décor
(Continued from page 52)

Row 5: P11, p2 tog, p4. (16 sts)
Row 6: K2, yo, k3tog, yo, k3, yo, k2, [ssk, yo] twice, k2. (17 sts)
Row 8: K2, yo, k2tog, yo, k1, [yo, k2, ssk] twice, yo, ssk, yo, k2. (19 sts)
Row 10: K2, yo, k2tog, yo, k3, yo, k2, [ssk] 3 times, yo, ssk, yo, k2. (19 sts)
Row 12: K2, [yo, k2tog] twice, k2, yo, k1, yo, [sl1, k2tog, psso] twice, ssk, yo, k2. (17 sts)
Row 13: P4, p2 tog-b, p11. (16 sts)
Row 14: K2, [yo, k2tog] twice, k2, yo, k3, yo, sl1, k2tog, psso, yo, k2. (17sts)
Row 16: K2, yo, k2tog, yo, [k2tog, k2, yo] twice, k1, yo, ssk, yo, k2. (19sts)
Repeat rows 1–16 until the desired length has been reached.
Cast (bind) off.

Making up

Make two rings in the same yarn, one for each end of the tie back. They should be large enough for the end to be sewn in place and then be hooked out of the way if wished. To make ring-work flowers, see page 128 and stitch into position.

Lampshade cover

Using 8.00mm (US 11) needles, cast on 98 sts.
Work open work insertion pattern 9 times.
Knit two rows, do not cast (bind) off.

Making up

Thread long length of yarn through yarn needle and thread through all sts, taking each one off knitting needle one by one. Pull tight, fasten and secure. At the same time, using same thread, sew up the two sides as neatly as possible.

Make a small (thumb size) ring from Embellishments (see page 128) with one round of buttonholing and stitch this to the top end of the lampshade. Add ringwork flowers as desired. Starch if desired before placing over a standard
lampshade cover. See diagram on previous page for placement.

Candlewick cushion
(Continued from page 62)

1. Come up at A and wrap thread around needle once in counterclockwise direction.

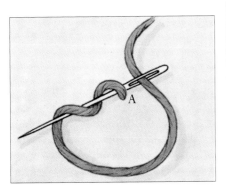

2. Wrap thread around needle a second time in same direction, keeping needle away from fabric.

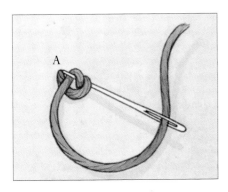

3. Push wraps together and slide to end of needle. Go down close to starting point, pulling thread through to form knot.

Rag rug sampler
(Continued from page 71)

Continue to alternate for variety until length desired is reached and begin centre parcel.

Using Biggy Print, knit 27.5cm (11in) of pattern D. Work opposite end of rug knitting same stitches in reverse order. The evenness and firmness of this rug can be improved by weaving. This bulks up the texture very quickly. Using the tapestry needle threaded with any of the yarns above, begin to weave in and out of the knitted stitches that show some thinness or are in need of some extra density.

The edges to this rug appear to be braided. In fact, a simple oversew stitch with the darning needle and the Biggy Print yarn from above was used doubled, carefully following the stitch line of the rug. This was repeated for both ends using Biggy Print, again matching sides with the same oversew stitch.

Finally, apply a simple fringe using the remainder of the Biggy Print and a small amount of a thin shiny yarn at each end of the rug. Add a tassel to each corner.

Making up
Block the completed rug, stretching it as tightly as possible. This will help to even out any discrepancies in the fabric. Cover it with a damp (not wet) colourfast towel and leave to dry. This will help the rug to memorize any changes, especially if it contains wool. Leave for a further 48 hours to 'set'.

Classic baby blanket
(Continued from page 74)

With size 3.25 mm (US 3) needles and 3 strands of yarn, cast on 8 sts (or more if a wider edge is desired) and work a band in garter st knit to edge all four sides. Using my joining technique, work beginning at a corner, as follows:
1 Knit to last st but one on needle, insert point of right hand needle into last st and at the same time insert this same point into an edge stitch of blanket.
2 Knit these two sts together, turn.
3 Yo, knit first two sts together.
4 Knit to end.
On completion of band cast (bind) off, secure neatly to the start of band.
Fold and slip stitch into place enclosing any raw edges.

Alternatively, continue knitting with the circular needle for a further 1.5cm (⅝in) and cast (bind) off. Press and slip stitch band into place, enclosing blanket edges.

Finishing
For each **square** sewn together, there are now parallel lines of purled stitches.

Turn blanket to WS and pick up 2–3 sts from one purled row on WS and 2–3 sts from purled row on opposite triangle of this square and stitch together. These picked up sts can be anywhere, as where they are positioned is what constitutes the pattern on the RS. In this cover they have been picked up ⅔rds along the bound off edge, giving an 'offset' look to the cover. Rep with all pieces to show up the special effects. Place Ringwork flowers at different points.

Garden plot counterpane
(Continued from page 82)

These can either be joined together with crochet, or every yarn over can be pressed open and then linked to its neighbour to achieve a similar look to crochet.

Thread a tapestry needle or similar with strands of A and enough length to complete one side of one square twice over. Matching each pair of loops exactly, overcast them together. Now, come back down the SAME side with the same overcast stitches – this will reverse the pattern of 'overs' you made on the previous row, giving a slight criss-cross effect. If this is done neatly it will give uniformity similar to crocheted work.

Edging

This counterpane has an ordinary garter st edge of 20 sts, knitted and joined with a Double Knot Fringe (see page 125) afterwards, but you can choose any edging from Embellishments.

The garter st edge can be any width. Use the following joining method to obtain a firm and machine edged look. Beginning at a corner, knit to last stitch but one, insert point of right hand needle into last stitch and at the same time pick up a loop from the counterpane. Knit last stitch and loop together. Turn. Yarn over (YO), knit next two stitches together and knit to end of row. Add fringe.

SQUARE DANCE

Make a cardboard template of the knitted square so that when you are blocking and pressing, the squares will all achieve the same overall size. Do not starch when pressing – because of the combination of plies, starching will not be effective.

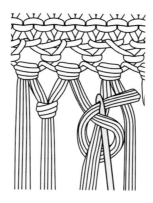

DOUBLE KNOT I

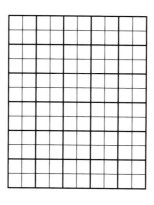

☐ SQUARE

▦ PANEL OF 4 SQUARES

Denim rug
(Continued from page 99)

Making up

Pin 2 I-cords in A and 2 I-cords in B together and anchor them to a secure position. Braid these four strands together and secure with an elastic band.

Remove the pin and tidy the ends by whipping or overcasting the ends. Coil the remaining I-cord in B neatly for the centre of the rug. After a few turns, and working from the back of the rug, begin to overcast or lace each turn. Then tuck the end of the braided I-cord neatly into one of the turns and begin to curl the braided I-cord. At the same time, continue to feed the single I-cord alongside. Using a large or lacing needle, sew each braid either by overcasting or lacing at regular intervals.

One strand of A and one of B were used together for the knitted edge. Once the circle of braided I-cord has been completed, attach the border of loop knitting and finally the edge of twice knit knitting.

Pin out rug as taut as possible into circular shape. Cover with a damp cloth and leave to dry.

Terms and abbreviations

K	Knit.
P	Purl.
St	Stitch. **Sts** – Stitches.
Tog	Together.
Sl	Slip a stitch or stitches by passing from the left hand needle to the right hand needle without working.
Dec	Decrease.
Inc	Increase.
M.st	Moss st.
Yf	Yarn forward.
Yb	Yarn back.
Yo	Yarn over.
[yo] twice	Double yarn over.
K1-b	Knit one stitch through its back loop, inserting the needle into the stitch from the right-hand side.
P1-b	Purl one stitch through its back loop, placing the right-hand needle point behind the back loop and purl the stitch as usual.
C6B	Cable 6 back slip next three stitches onto a cable needle and hold at back of work. Knit next 2 stitches from left hand needle, then knit stitches from cable needle.
Sl-st	A stitch that has been slipped.
Psso	Pass slipped stitch over.
MB	(Make a bobble) Knit into front and back and front of next stitch. Turn and purl three turn and k.3, turn and p1, ptog, turn and k2tog.
Rep	Repeat.
Rep from *	Repeat all instructions that come after the *, in the same order.
[] Brackets	Those instructions within the brackets must be repeated as often as is specified immediately after the brackets.
Ssk	Slip, slip, knit (sl1, k1, psso).

K2tog	Knit two stitches together.
P2tog	Purl two stitches together.
K2togtbl	Insert needle into the back two loops of two stitches together and then kit them together to make one.
P2togtbl	Insert needle into back two loops of the second and first stitches and them purl them together.
Inc	Make an extra stitch by either a) Knitting into the front and then the back of the stitch, or b) Purling into the front and back of the stitch.
M1	Make One. Increase by inserting the needle below the thread passing between the two immediate stitches, lifting the thread with the left hand needle and knitting into the back of it.
To Knit below	Place right hand needle into the loop below the next stitch on the left hand needle and not into the loop on the needle.
Yo	Yarn Over. Bring the yarn over the top of the needle once before knitting the next stitch also.
WRN	Wool round needle.
WF	Wool forward.
Turn	Turn the knitting round before the end of the row.
Short row	This is the knitting completed after a turn.
Dpn	Double pointed needles.
St st	Stocking stitch. Knit all right side rows, purl all wrong side rows.
Reverse St st	Reverse Stocking stitch. Purl right side rows, knit all wrong side rows.

Resources

UNITED KINGDOM

Louet/Euroflax
Kwinkweerd 139
7241 CW Lochem
+31 573 252229
www.louet.nl

Rowan
Green Lane Mill
Holmfirth
HD9 2DX England
+ 44 (0) 1484 681881
www.knitrowan.com

Yeoman Yarn
36 Churchill Way
Fleckney
Leicestershire
England
LE8 8UD
+44 (0) 116 2404464
www.yeoman-yarns.co.uk

Andru Knitwear
PO Box 35
Brampton
Cumbria
England
CA8 7YA
+44 (0) 169 7747571

UNITED STATES

Louet/Euroflax
808 Commerce Park Drive
Ogdensburg, NY 13669
+ 1 (613) 925-4502
+ 1 (613) 925-1405
info@louet.com

Rowan
Distributed by Westminster Fibers
4 Townshend West
Unit 8
Nasuha, NH 03063
www.knitrowan.com

Yeoman Yarn
1730 Abilene Street
Suite 102
Aurora, CO 80012
(800) YARN-UPS

CANADA

Louet
R.R. 4
Prescott, ONT K0E 1T0

Rowan
Distributed by Diamond Yarn
9697 St. Laurent, Suite 101
Montreal, QC H3L 2N1
www.knitrowan.com

Yeoman Yarn
Distributed by Cardiknits
92 Cardinal Drive
Hamilton, ONT
LA9 4H7

Project index

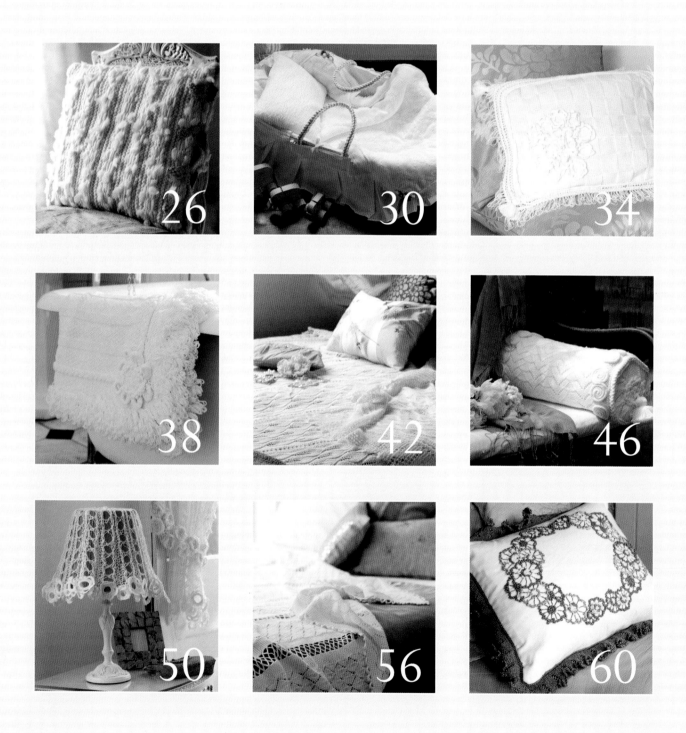

26

30

34

38

42

46

50

56

60

64

68

72

76

80

84

88

92

96

100

106

Acknowledgements

This book is dedicated to Dr. Sam McNamara who will be sadly missed.

Maureen Acland OBE who is a truly gracious person and has given me such amazing support over the years. Gladys Russell who has been a wonderful nursing colleague. And last, but certainly not least, to all my grandchildren: Chloe, Ophelia, Elliot, Alex, Nathalie Jane, Rufus, and Roma.

Acknowledgements to Marie Clayton, for her faith in my endeavours and without whom I would never have reached this stage. Debbie Abrahams – for her patience, help, and kindness. I'd also like to extend my gratitude to Heather Esswood, Laura Johnson, Ann Kemp, Michelle Lo, Katie Hudson and Helen McCarthy for their generosity of spirit and goodwill.

For more information about this book, visit www.heirloomknits.com.